Seven Names Off The Wall

The True Story of The Flight of Spooky 71 By The Pilot Who Flew It

BY

FRANK SLOCUM

CONTENTS

AUTHOR'S DEDICATION

First and foremost, "Seven Names Off the Wall" is dedicated to my family, my late wife Cheryl Lynn, daughters Courtney, Kyleigh, and Whitney, and grandchildren who never would have been.

Second, to the members of my Spooky Brotherhood who served at the call of our nation.

Third, for all the men and women who answered the call in all wars, risking life, limb, and mind, unsung heroes who saw their duty before them. Finally, for the over 50,000 casualties whose names are etched into the Vietnam Memorial and we can lightly trace them with reverence for their spirits. They are never forgotten.

Fourth, to the widows and families, who stand facing the black onyx, fighting tears, answered silently back by the warriors who silently stand with their comrades, linked arm in arm for history.

FOREWORD

I was honored when asked by Frank Slocum to serve as a copy editor and scrutineer of this book. I have known Frank Slocum for many years – Several years longer than I have been married, and that approaches fifty years. Yet it was only recently that I learned his middle name.

Frank and I flew missions together for many months in Thailand, and he was the only "crew" I was ever assigned with in my entire flying career. I always felt safe when flying with Frank. As competent as any flyer I met during my time. I'd do it again in a heartbeat. My next assignment, Military Airlift Command (MAC), in its infinite wisdom and today's airlines, did not fly "crews" but flew each man individually as they came up in the flying rotation queue. With a dedicated crew, we knew what each crew member thought and how he would react under stress.

But I digress. This is the true story surrounding the USAF's first Medal of Honor given to an Enlisted Airman during our involvement in Viet Nam – the back story.

Frank has never wavered in his telling me about Levitow, Carpenter, et al., And I often asked for expanded details. On the other hand, my war stories get better with each telling.

Mark Steetle
Captain, USAF
Spooky Navigator

CHAPTER 1
IT ALL BEGINS

Newark Airport, September 1968

My Mom and Dad were there, seeing me off, boarding a Braniff flight for San Francisco, and on to Viet Nam. Most of us had loaded, and with final hug and kisses, boarding pass in hand, I headed for the door, the attendant took my pass, and I turned a last time to say goodbye, a wave, and dressed in my service tan uniform, through the door I went.

My mothers' thoughts were "That is the last we will see of him…"

How did I get there…

Frank Heidl Slocum, Jr., was born in Westfield, New Jersey, June of 1943, while Frank's dad was in the army, having been drafted early in 1942. He was a corporate sales manager for a small import and distribution company in New York City. His mother had been a grade school teacher in the Westfield school system. An older draftee at 40 years of age, his father had been assigned to the Army Supply Depot in Bayonne, New Jersey, virtually commuting distance from his home town, and where the Slocums rented an upstairs apartment on Temple Place. It also was a block away from his parents' house on Summit Avenue in Westfield.

1

Franks father remained in the Army until 1944, when he was discharged as an older veteran, married, with one child. Returning to his old job, the Slocums found a home on Mountain Avenue in Westfield. The home was about a 15-year-old model home, built among established neighbors. To the right were the Dukay's, and the left a large victory garden, owned by the Wilson's, whose house was next to it. The garden and field were complete with a raspberry patch, coop and chickens. It was a neighborhood where everybody knew each other and contributed to the war effort.

Frank's dad, who went by his Germanic middle name, Heidl, fit right into the neighborhood and spent untold hours laboring on the property, to bring it to his liking. Frank Heidl Jr., fit right in as a toddler and was soon joined, in 1946, with a younger brother, Ray. As they grew up, they were somewhat mischievous, but well-liked boys.

The Wilson's kept their acre sized Victory Garden even after the war. And the neighbors were invited to use it. Now it is important to note that the Wilsons had three boys, Jim, who joined the post war Navy, and Tom and Billy, who joined the Air Force. Billy was a spirited boy, who in his college school years would drive young Frank Heidl around in circles on the fallow garden in the rumble seat of his model A Ford. He would also, while holding his hands, twirl him around and around. Tom also did well and became an architect and stayed in the Air Force Reserves.

Moving forward five years, about 1954, Korea had wound down, and the word around the summer neighborhood, "Billy is Coming", Billy

Wilson was going to buzz his home. Billy had graduated from college, completed Air Force Pilot Training and had become an Air Force flight instructor.

Billy and a pilot trainee had stayed overnight at McGuire Air Base near Mt. Holly, NJ. It was part of a cross country flight regimen. Probably another Jersey Boy. It was an easy 50-mile trip to overfly Westfield, NJ.

The neighborhood was ready. A number of neighbors came over into our back yard because vision was better. Bath and beach towels were laid out in a pattern on the grass in our yard. Folks were standing around. We kids were all excited, and every plane on a Newark departure flight path would strike our interest. "Is that Billy?" No, now wait.

Soon a buzz went through the group. He was coming, anticipation arose. In a few seconds a polished Air Force T-33 two seat trainer zoomed over with a roar at about 200 feet, just above the tree tops to us. To me it was awe inspiring, "Wow!!" jumping up and down. The plane made an abrupt climbing left turn, wings rocking, climbing, climbing to the west. Such a morning, right then I decided, "That is what I want to do...!"

Years later Billy and I spoke about the flyover. He laughed and said "Teaching my student how to break all the rules and regulations". When asked about the wing rocking, "That was so no one could get my numbers". No one would ever turn in a Wilson boy, let alone Billy.

About that time in life, another aircraft flight caught my eye. It was a Saturday morning and my cousin and I were in the front yard when a flight of four, four ship formations of Flying Wings flew over at relatively low altitude, enroute from Republic Aviation on Long Island to their demise and destruction on the western desert. Their demise was all political, led by a Texas Senator, who funded a short-lived B-36 bomber. Such a waste of technology that took 50 years to recover.

Time moved on and I attended and graduated from Westfield Senior High. I was never a great grade student, rather preferring to attend auto shop and then stay and work after school building a unique two-cylinder go-cart engine. I never really finished it, but I learned about the operation of most every machine shop machine. My actual learning experience was significant.

However, I did score well on the SAT tests, and Dean **Walter Cox** at Clemson admissions must have seen something and sent me a positive admissions notice. Why Clemson? Because it did not look old and stogy, and with no ivy on the buildings. Weeks later I learned there were no female students, only men. August of 1961, I started at Clemson as a "Rat", the lowest of life on campus. Clemson had previously been an all-male military college, and a shaved head and "Dink" hat were "A rigor" for all rats. But I lucked out again and was housed on the first floor, "F" dorm, room "F-114" among athletic upperclassmen. Giant football players and basketball players who had to duck to pass through a door way were my neighbors. I was the only rat on the floor.

As a rat, I quickly learned to adapt and gained their protection. There was a wonderful, mushy "Whopper" like hamburger place downtown, "Dan's" the place in the community, where I would go to very night at ten PM. Moving from door to door in the dorm, I would ask "Anything from Dan's", those that wanted anything would give me a couple dollars, and their order. In those days I would then run downtown, await their large orders an bring them back in a carton for delivery. "Thanks, Rat", and on to the next room. Protection.

First, Rats were dumb as stones. And about 50% dropped out by Thanksgiving. Gone, done. Really. I was scared, but had a Westfield, NJ education. One fact was my freshman math book was the exact same one I had in high school, and my copious history notes worked well also. I became a 3.0 B student.

Now Rats were tormented by some upper-class men. They were supposed to sing, chant, dance on tables, carry dinner trays back to the dump belt, and often run like an unending snake through the dining hall and around campus. I would go to the chow hall and always sat in between athlete hall mates. The athletes were all well-known on campus, so when approached by an upperclassman to join the festivities, a hand would be placed on my shoulder "No, he stays, he is our rat". So, I survived. I also carried their trays back to the belt. Humility counts.

Another very important thing I learned was how to play bridge. My next door neighbor was also a non-athlete, but a junior upper class man. Every day we would watch Johnny Carson "You Bet Your Life" at 4PM in the cool dark lounge. Our sleeping rooms in the "Tin Cans", alleged temporary dorms, were not. Temporary, they were not, as the last of them lived on 50 years. One room should have been memorialized in the Smithsonian.

Then at 8PM, there would be a bridge game in his room. I was able to escape at ten, saying I had a "Dan's Run" to make in the first semester. Plus, my hair was growing out. However, I did learn bridge that would carry me in later life. My studies suffered, but my life learning experiences did not.

I had joined Air Force ROTC, so had to wear a uniform on Thursdays and learn to march around the field in front of the main campus hall. I actually like marching and my ROTC studies. For freshmen, two years were mandatory then, either Air Force or Army, and I had my plans. I indicated my interest in the Air Force as a career, and stayed on in ROTC two more years. I enjoyed my classes and gave a big report on Laos, which served me well later. Only recently did Laos get a railroad.

Because I changed majors, I ended up spending an extra year at Clemson, 5 years (Thanks Dad) graduating with 160 credits. My life changed the last two years, attending only about half the classes, preferring to travel to Washington, DC, to be with my most favored girlfriend. My GPA slipped, but I floated it enough to graduate.

I also topped out the GRE "Graduate Record Exam", mandatory at Clemson as a measure of their learning effectiveness, another well spent day, that caught the eye of at least one Dean. I told him it must be your tests that didn't measure learning. I was dismissed to wander about a week before graduation and commissioning in the Air Force. A butter bar Lieutenant I was to be.

One other ROTC benefit was the Flight Instruction Program, or "FIP", where I learned to fly about in a Cessna 172 for about 30 hours and soloing. I can't say I loved it, but learned a good lesson about "Getting Lost". I was supposed to fly to Greenwood airport solo, land, have them sign my log book and return. Well, I failed to plan it well, which I now view as a program deficiency, and got entirely lost. Lost big time. I saw an interstate highway, "Concrete Airways" as they became known as, and I went down real low, probably scaring travelers, and read the road sign "Donaldson AFB", so I know knew where I was, made a hard left turn and headed back, heading down I-85. I sort of knew the roads, and turned right later and spying the new Lake Hartwell, and the campus, and landed across the lake at the airfield. No one was around, so I tied the plane down and left. No one ever signed, or saw, my log book. It was a well learned lesson, that I finally made up for in my low-level Air Force T-38 300 knot per hour training.

My parents attended graduation and commissioning. I was now on my own. I had an option to postpone active duty for ten months, and I was tired of studies. I took the option and headed for Washington, DC.

DC Days

I had spent two summers previously in Washington, and really enjoyed it. OK, it was because of a girl that I met in Westfield and thought she was "The One". But she was a little unsettled, but still very much there. She was attending Geo. Washington U., a year junior to me. She was also my next door neighbor.

I interviewed a few companies at Clemson, but my course was set—Military in ten months. I did get an offer to join GM Cadillac Division, a great starting job. Detroit which would have been home base. However, I knew not a soul there, and get an apartment? So, I declined. Today I wonder where it would have taken me.

And as I had done in the summers, looked on Georgetown University bulletin boards. "Roommate Wanted" by two grad students, furnished, caught my eye. Visited, good deal and I said yes. Now for a job. I went to DC, moved into the shared apartment, Georgetown, 18th Street, at Pennsylvania Avenue.

I looked through the "Positions" in the Washington Post, and saw one "Ass't to Chief Engineer", Alexandria, VA. It listed an address, and I went. Now it was not that easy because I had no car. It was on a bus route. Off I bussed, transfers, changed busses and travelled down Route 1, eyeing the address numbers. Got close and walked a hundred feet. There it was, "Value Engineering Company". It was about three in the afternoon. I went in, got a visitors pass and was taken before a nice lady in Personnel. She asked about a resume. What resume? I just graduated, but did air conditioning work summers. She took some notes. "Excuse me, I'll be back", and left. Now a talent gained by the best of salesmen is reading notes upside down. So, I read hers, "Young" College grad" "Gregarious". Maybe it was because I wore my only jacket, a Madras Plaid, in at the time.

Soon she returned with a gentleman, "This is Pete Magarelli, and he'd like to talk to you". We went off and talked, Pete was easy going and told me what he wanted. Basically, some overflow help. I responded positively. He thanked me and left. She soon returned and made me a job offer, I took it, basically at about $1500 a month. Not great, but kept the rain off my head. I started in a day or two. Their day started at 7AM, so I would get a DC bus to 14th Street at five AM, and having a transfer slip, could, get off, go into a breakfast spot, have some eggs, and then get on a VA bus to work, arriving a little before seven.

All worked out well, and my new boss, Pete would drive me back to DC on his way home evenings in Maryland. So, I had a chance to talk and learn from him. My first assignment was in the metallurgy lab making samples and polishing them. They were pieces of ship missile launch pads, and the samples were used to evaluate wear. After a couple of months, I was moved upstairs, near Pete, title" Junior Engineer", and a dollar an hour raise. I was hourly because of the way that the government was billed under contract. I had some blueprint experience at Clemson, and so, Pete would hand me a stack of drawings and say, "I'll get back to you". Never did. Basically, they were Naval ship missiles, and I had to see if they would fit together. Oh, I had to get a "Secret" clearance, which was soon issued after a little paperwork.

Pete and I worked out a system, and he was always surprised when I came to him "All done, marked up" in about 80% of the allowed time.

I competed against U of MD graduate engineers, and quite frankly waxed them. They didn't know which end if a screwdriver to use. I got better projects. Value Engineering was a military engineering company, and in 1966, supporting Vietnam war projects. Pete handed me one, the structure to mount JATO rocket assist motors to a C130 aircraft for short field boosted take offs. My Clemson flight experiences came into play as I understood minimum in-flight airspeeds.

And since I was so efficient, and had time left over, others were logged into my projects, because they were slow, or overwhelmed.

With my new wealth, three months into the job, I bought my first Corvette, a blue, 1964, two-year old coupe. A truly great car that I had to sell when I left for Vietnam. I wish I had it now.

My girlfriend and I grew closer, and we spent every day together. It was a glorious time. The only time we were apart was when we would drive to Westfield and go to each other's respective homes.

The ten months moved quickly, only so many hot fudge Sundaes at the Hot Shoppes to be had. On the day of departure, she wanted to pack and go with me. I told her no, she had another year to go in college, and the Air Force was anticipating a bachelor officer. But, if she wanted to get married in route, we could make it work. I was ready, and she was not. Departing, a wave, and it was the last I saw of her. I was off to pilot training.

Quite by an accident of fate, a young man sat down next to her on a train trip home, a few months later, a fellow Westfielder I knew, and she, quite frankly, fell head over heels for him, he met all her criteria for a mate and husband. They married, and fifty years later, had four children. I missed her terribly, but now support her totally, she made the right decision in life.

CHAPTER 2
PILOT TRAINING

I received my first set of military orders, report to Undergraduate Pilot Training (UPT), 10 May 1967, Randolph AFB, Universal City, Texas. Class 68-G.

I left Washington DC about five days prior, on a Wednesday, stopped overnight in Columbus, Ohio, and then again near Dallas Texas. The car was loaded, and cruised effortlessly. Day three, I entered the gates at Randolph, showed my orders, asked directions, and found the Housing Office. Randolph is of Spanish architecture, and very orderly.

I showed my orders to the housing staff and was sent to a two-story bachelor officer quarters, (BOQ). I was on the second floor. It was very hot, so I brought up only a few items, the rest could wait for evening. There was a second story walkway around the building, and I walked to the other side and leaned on the railing. Every few minutes a white jet, or two, would pass by over the runway area. Now, Friday afternoon, about 3 PM. I saw it, a plume of black smoke rose to my left, at where I guessed the runway began, a half mile away. I was impressed. All quiet, but ominous, nothing. I kept watching and soon the white airplanes re-appeared. I watched for a while, perhaps half an hour, and again this significant plume reappeared. Hmm, I thought, "This may not be so easy". I retired to my air-conditioned quarters, and put my feet up. Two bedrooms, but no roommate.

A little bored, I studied my base map and found the Officers Club. Dinner, why not. The club is a very Class A Spanish design club, and later because it was the Headquarters, for the Air Training Command (ATC), deserved special attention. Friday night, a little early, I studied my surroundings, and would see well-dressed men and women enter, and some uniforms, Generals, Colonels, Majors, all passing through. And also, some younger men on these really neat, zipper laden, polished black boots, flight suits. I was impressed. I was in civilian dress. Finally, I went into the dining room and had a nice dinner.

My orders specified Base Theater, 1PM, on Sunday. Most had their tan uniforms. Anyway, I found my way there, and the room filled with about 90 young officers, all seated. Soon the room was called to attention and officers mounted the stage. It was my first call to attention. We then were seated and various speakers approached the podium to welcome us, Class 68-G, the first Randolph AFB undergraduate class since WWII. The very first. "First and Finest" became our motto.

Finally, a full colonel addressed us. A full Colonel, an officer with Eagles on his shoulders. The senior Officer, as Generals were above him. Later regarded as a really neat guy, and he made General. He welcomed us, two squadrons, 45 students to each. Then he dropped "the bomb" on us. However, he emphasized, "This will not be easy" and "less than half of you will graduate to become Air Force pilots."

Wow!!" For whatever reasons, they will go on elsewhere. I turned to the fellows on the left and right of me, and said "Don't bother unpacking". And thought, maybe that now explains the black smoke plumes.

Now I must interject here, a young candidate, Ed Pechnik. AKA "Fast Eddy", was at a different point, also viewing the smoke plumes and thinking similar thoughts.

Ed and I became best pals, and later chuckled at finding that the plumes were from Fire Rescue training at an old fuselage off in a corner of the base.

CESSNA T-41

First training was in a military version of a Cessna 172, which I had flown, called a T-41. No back seat, and 5 horsepower more than a 172. We were bussed daily by squadron, to Stinson Field near San Antonio for training by civilian pilots. I had an old experienced pilot, little grouchy. I did everything well except power on stalls, which I considered unskilled. I think I got a check eval ride from the head instructor. Not good. But I developed a technique, of backing off the throttle undetected about a quarter inch, and with the wheel almost full back, jerk on it which would cause the plane to stall in the air, and the nose fall, usually breaking right, opposite of prop rotation. Recovery was easy. I had to demonstrate stall left, right and straight ahead. If I used full power, the nose would just hang and fly around. I never did try, full power and jerking on the wheel. I passed, and on to jet training. Over ten classmates, maybe 12, did not.

THE "TWEET" A T37 TRAINER

The Air Force T37 jet trainer was another Cessna product. It had been around for a while. Twin engine, student and instructor seated side by side. Ejection seats and a clamshell canopy. The plane was close to the ground, so we just climbed in.

Why the "Tweet"? Because the twin centrifugal jet engines made a loud screeching noise at idle, so everyone including the ground crew had to wear ear protectors, and ear plugs, coming and going, otherwise hearing loss-thus, the tweet name.

We were delivered to the flight line, and our plane, in an Air Force "Bread Truck" as they were fondly known. A bench box seat along the wall. We had a check list, a strap on knee pad, all in a helmet bag. We also carried a parachute, usually over our shoulder. And issue sun glasses. We were "Cool".

It was here we first learned to read the "781", a maintenance document on the airplane, and how to do a walkaround basic inspection. Check the nose gear, panels closed, check the light lenses, look in the engine exhausts, do the "You Who" check as I called it. Oh yes, wear flying gloves, real leather flight gloves.

Arrive at the airplane, look at the last three tail numbers to make sure it is your plane, put you parachute in the plane and placed on the seat. Arrange the straps. Put your checklist, open to "starting engines" and your knee pad, on the left dash, helmet on the canopy rail, hook up the oxygen mask hose to the regulator, look to see that the ejection seat pins were in place with the tell-tale ribbons. Make sure the gear lever is in the down position. Look around inside and check for snakes. (This was Texas!) Aux power was usually hooked up and running, so the running lights were on. Look at the 781 to see the comments of the last fliers. Flip to the "Yellow pages" in the rear and look for deferred maintenance. The 781 binder went on the other seat.

Then do your walk around. Many "New-be" students carried their yellow checklists as they did their walk around. Most learned quickly.

There was an early on tale, usually presented by upperclassmen, to never bail out without the 781 binder, because it had all the aircraft records. Some thought it true.

Pilots should have pulled the gear locking pins as a part of their walk around.

Then approach the cockpit area, looking to make sure the seat cushion was in place, parachute centered. Left foot into the foot well, one hand on the ejection seat, the other on the windshield rail. Boost yourself in, both feet together, and turning, so as to bring them down in front of your seat, together. Sit back.

One of the reasons for the strenuous Air Force PT was to be able to accomplish a graceful entrance. The other is to not break a pilot's rule. **Bold face "Do not step on the seat cushion"**. The casual reader might think "Why?". Again, learned from pilot experience, there is invariably jet fuel droplets on the hardtop, and that will get on the soles of your boots. Step on the cushion and it will transfer to it. About 30 minutes into flight, you will think someone has taken a blowtorch to your perinium There is no place to stand up.

Usually, the ground crewmen will help with the parachute straps and the five-point seat straps. A little wiggle and you are in place.

Remember your helmet on the canopy rail. Now is a good time to reach over your left shoulder, retrieve it, and put it on. Invariably, some new over anxious student tries to lower the canopy, crunching and splitting their helmet. Not a good start. Your ear protector goes on the rudder pedal height adjustment knob shaft. By now the instructor is in the plane, the 781 folder is deposited in the storage box beside him.

Ready to start engines. Give a finger twirl, reach down and lift the start engine switch and hold on. Move the left throttle the start engine position, watch the exhaust gas temp needle rise, indicating combustion. Lift the throttle over center and wait for idle stabilization. Do the same for engine two.

Look over at the ground chief and give him, or her, vertical, fingers up, a thumb and finger "Quack-quack" signal and move the speedbrake switch forward and aft. A nod usually indicates proper activation. Then a hinged clapping signal, and move the flap lever to the up position. Again, a nod. A good time to look at hydraulic pressure in the green.

There are mirrors on the forward windshield rails. Adjust your seat and them so you can see the rudder. Pull the control stick back and you will see the elevator rise. Forward, down elevator. Rudder pedal left and right to check it. If you did a good job on your walk around, and lifted the elevator to the neutral position, you can check the trim tab. Usually a little nose up trim, will make the take off smoother. Click the trim button back twice.

Then look left and move the stick left. The aileron should move to the full up position. Move the stick to the right and it will go down. Glance over to the right and ensure the aileron is full up.

With experience, a pilot can do all the above faster than it took to read the paragraphs. Give the ground chief two thumbs out and the chocks will be pulled, and a little throttle and the plane can move. Do a quick visual for equipment left or right. There is a little button near your pinky finger. Press and hold it and move the rudder pedals left or right and the plane will turn.

If you have set your radio knob to stop one, a quick call lets ground control know you are taxiing. If an instructor is with you, you use his call sign, if solo, you have your unique call sign. Your call sign will also indicate you class and experience level. It is a good time to hook the red emergency parachute pull hook, necessary for a very early ejection.

Your first flight in the tweet will be a demo ride. Consider yourself lucky if you get twenty minutes of "Stick" time. Usually greatly over controlled, as you learn through experience, airplanes at speed are controlled by pressure, not movement.

Perhaps four more classmates will drop out at this point.

The landing pattern is interesting. Unlike civilian aircraft that fly an exaggerated pattern of left and right turns, finally lining up with the runway, military patterns are tight ovals designed to get the most aircraft down in the shortest period of time. To do this a turn called a "Pitch out" is used. The pilot flies down the runway centerline about a third of a mile, at a thousand feet of altitude, and then with an abrupt pull in the stick, initiates a roll to 60 degrees, and enough back pressure and rudder to hold altitude. Which way you pitch depends on which runway one is using, either left or right. Right runway pitch right. Left pitch left, usually.

Hold the turn until you have completed 180 degrees of turn, and you have reversed your course. You are now flying parallel to the run way. Time for gear handle down. Once down, and you are about 45 degrees off the end of the runway, flaps down, and throttle reduced, initiate a turn to line up with the runway. This is where experience comes into play.

The secret is to look way out when you have reversed your course and try to spot something on the horizon, a barn, a building, a tree, whatever and stay left or right of the object. When the object gets in the right position, initiate your turn and descent, and see where it takes you. If you don't like it, make a low approach and go around. Pull too tight in your turn and you could stall and crash.

About four or five leave the program, as they just could not master the gear down, flaps, turn, descend.

After about ten flights, 10 to 12 hours of time, demonstrating some skill in the air, you are ready to solo, go it alone. Usually, the instructor tells you to taxi back by the mobile observation station, and he just gets out. Ok, you are on your own now. The joke on me was, and I never did live it down, "Do you want me to come back and pick you up?"

The first jet solo is like loss of virginity. It just sort of comes at you. Lift off and you are on your own. One generally stays in the pattern, flying a box pattern, trying to remember the sequence of events taking place, gear, flaps, turn, and trying to spot elusive distant point. The joke always was "If the farmer learns you are using his tree, he'll chop it down." No shame in going around if you don't like the approach, but at some point, you are going to have to land.

Three or four more leave the program, "Fear of flight".

So, OK. Meet your instructors. Your class is divided into two squadrons, "A" and "B". When you were not flying, you would have academics. So "A" would fly mornings for a week, and the groups would flip and "B" would fly mornings. Some days you both would fly.

There were only so many instructors for the pre-solo phase. I flew with **Major Anthony Farrington**, whose college degree was in Music Appreciation. Now don't belittle that, as he had been an F-105 pilot flying missions over North Viet Nam, one of the most dangerous missions of the entire war effort. I did not appreciate that until I had actually served there.

There was one of many who stood out. **Major Emil Vollmar,** from Upstate New York, who was like a "Gun Slinger" from olden days. A larger-than-life character, he was Squadron Operations Officer. Allegedly, he had left the service and came back in so he could go to Viet Nam and bomb and strafe. He had a booming voice, and all listen when he spoke. He also had an infectious chuckle when describing stupid students.

Now nearing winter, the fog would roll up from the Gulf mornings and blanket the area. It was known as "Scud". The bottom was about 500 feet above the ground to 2000 feet at the top, and sunny above. It would burn off by 11AM.

No Solo flying. Advanced students could go up with an instructor for instrument indoctrination. A preview of instrument flying. When we were not flying, Major Vollmar would give us his personal indoctrination, often leaning on the podium, and chuckling.

"If your airplane is on fire, and you had no control, and it is Sunday morning and heading for the Catholic Church, bail out, as there is no good reason to join the pyre. And if you had any control, you'd hit the Baptists." And "If you are taking off, lose engines, and are settling down, put the throttles to the firewall and beyond. There is no good reason to try to 'Save the Engines'. Now the low experience National Airline pilots, taking off from Washington National on an icy winter day, could have done that when engine pressure sensors iced over. The plane would have jumped into the air by advancing throttles, instead of settling into the Potomac River. And if they had used engine "heat" from the start, nothing would have happened.

My favorite was "Last thing before bailing out, stop cock the engines (Shut Off), as it is very embarrassing to have the airplane keep flying around, and they have to send someone up to shoot it down."

And so, first day at our new training building, as we walked towards the classroom, there was a list of instructor names, and student last names. Top of the list was "Vollmar" and a note "Know all Acro maneuvers and entry airspeeds".

FIRST DAY!

I few with Vollmar a few times and loved it. He let you fly the plane. When you got to the flight area, just say "I'm ready" and commence with maneuvers, and do them one after another. Stalls, slow flight, acro and spins. What are spins? That is where you stall the aircraft in low-speed flight, hold the stick full back and apply full rudder. An obscene maneuver. The airplane will begin to rotate, with the nose rising and falling, it is no longer flying, it is falling. To stop it, apply full opposite rudder, holding the stick full back. The plane will stop rotating, and start to go in the opposite direction. At that point, move the stick full forward. The nose will drop, and forward flight at slow airspeed will begin. Ease the stick back and begin flying. Come back too fast, and it will begin a series of stairstep stalls.

This is what killed young Kennedy and friends. Even though he was flying in weather and clouds, if he had simply let go of the wheel, his Cessna would have resumed flying. Instead, confused by vertigo, he held the wheel back, and more than likely turned the wheel, opposing he pilot inexperienced vertigo. He spun all the way into the ocean.

One maneuver that I liked was a "Cloverleaf". West Texas had lots of North South and East West roads, so look out and pick one out. Go to full throttle, and lower the nose. When you get to about 275 knots, note your altitude, and begin a firm climb, loading the plane to about two and a half times gravity, 2 and ½ G's. Look left and right to make sure you are climbing straight up. Slowly, and smoothly unload the plane, ending at the top inverted and at one G. Using the rudder, and in slow flight, turn the plane 90 degrees, and start down, using the perpendicular road. As the plane speeds up, the load will increase, and by modulating the force, you want to end up at the bottom at about your starting altitude and airspeed. Do the same again, but this time turn in the opposite direction. Make four loops.

A word of caution. Always maintain about one G of force. If you go to zero "G's" inverted, every piece of loose crap, screws, washers, rocks and grit will move to the canopy. When you load the plane, it will fall on the IP and irritate him.

Final thoughts, it was fun to go to full power, accelerate, and climb. Take your ear protector off the rudder pedal handle, hold it in front of you and give it a spin, simultaneously pushing the nose over. The ear protector will be weightless, and spin. You can fly it with the stick and is good for about ten seconds of fun.

A final serious note, alcohol and flying. The rule is 12 hours. But one Friday, several of us stayed late at the club, thinking for sure no Saturday flying because of poor weather. The next morning, hung over, we got up at six, drank coffee and headed for the squadron building. Sure enough, we were to fly solo. Preflight, takeoff, all went fine. Now all of us monitor the same radio frequencies, "Student Common". I decided to do a loop. Well, pulling about three G's, my vision tunneled down to black. I unloaded the pull, and rolled to level. Whoa, that was not good. Alcohol depletes oxygen and, because of altitude and the night before drinking, and G forces, effectively blinded myself. I want over to 100 oxygen, and cold called to my buddy Ed Pechnik, who was also up and about, "Don't do any acro", to his response, "I know". Rest of the time, flew around, came back, landed and, logged our time. Lesson learned, never spoke of it again...

About four more students left the program, never could solo, or couldn't master the descending turn into final for landing. Our ranks were diminishing.

I did have a little problem with Instrument flying practice. The T-37 landing light. One was supposed to turn on the light for final and landing. To do so, the pilot flipped the switch, located on the left instrument panel to "Up" position. And on a touch and go, or go around, turn the light off by putting the switch in the down position. If you left it in the up position (On), and went to speed, it would bend the light bracket and maintenance didn't like that. So, I got written up for that.

I decided to put in a "Suggestion" with an argument to simply reverse the switch, as I knew others had the same problem. Up would be off and down would be on.

About a month later, I received a reply "Aircraft practice is that switches were to be in the "Down' position for off and "Up" for on. Thank you." I suspect T-37 brackets are still being bent.

NORTHROP T-38 "THE WHITE ROCKET"

Thanksgiving had passed, and it was midway between Thanksgiving and Christmas break. We were heavy into simulator training and blindfold cockpit exercises. Really not blindfolded, rather eyes closed. I would do before starting engine checking, sweeping from left to right, feeling every circuit breaker, switch, knob, position, hands on, gloves on, identifying them without looking.

And then the emergency procedures, Bold Face have to know without thinking. At 500 miles an hour, things happen fast. You should never hear the third call for bailout. "Arming handles raise, position, firing triggers, squeeze" Gone.

I learned a lot of techniques. I did not advance my throttles together, but separated, as I wanted to feel the "Bump-bump" of the afterburners turning on. I didn't need to look at anything, I just felt the airplane. In 20 seconds, you would be doing 330 miles an hour, gear up, flaps up, a thousand feet off the ground. Throttles out of afterburner, and forward a tad, and you are going 300 knots, 350 On the formation mph, ready for the first climbing turn out of the pattern. Things happen fast.

Now to the squadron room, and joined by another pilot candidate, I met for the first time my primary instructor, **Major Robert E. Turnbaugh**. He looked over my paperwork, saying, "Westfield, New Jersey, eh?" and Slocum. He then named my father, as I nodded. "He used to drive Billy Wilson and me to the train station on his way to work, " and "on rainy days drop us at school." Small world, he had two boys and had married a Westfield girl. He taught me how to really fly.

The T-38 is a supersonic twin engine jet. The instructor sits in a matching cockpit behind the student. It is an airborne sports car. And things can happen fast. The system has pass-fail check rides at regular intervals. It takes about ten one and a half hour flights, with real emphasis on the pattern and landing. By this time in the program, on a clear day, any student can fly it in a straight line. It is the pattern downwind and turn to final that are the separators. We lost another 10 students in this final phase, most due to "Fear of Flight", and some never could co-ordinate it all.

There was a window box with wheels out near the runway. It had air-conditioning and radios, binoculars and also a bright red-light signal light. Every day an instructor and a student manned "Mobile". It was a good time to get to really know your instructor and his stories.

A student would call in "'Call Sign Initial". Each class had a unique call sign name series and each student had a number. Mine was "Mojac 36". Likewise, the instructor had a name and number, then you could tell who was solo or dual.

Pick up the binoculars and look at the airplane. What one is looking for is "wheels down" just before the sweeping turn to final. Look closer for "flaps down", the square panels on the back side of the wings. Half flaps change the shape and airflow over the wings, allowing for the same lift at a slower airspeed. Full flaps increase the drag, allowing for descent.

The student should reduce thrust a little, start turn and allow the airplane to begin descent. A little rudder at this point will bring the nose around to avoid an overshoot, aiding in runway alignment. A quick peek at the altimeter, and rate of descent will tell the tale. One trap one does not want to get into is reducing power. Power is altitude, pitch nose up or down is airspeed. One does not want to get behind the "Power curve" in a jet, waiting for the engine to spool up. If you are a little high, sneak the speed brake out for a couple of seconds to reduce altitude. Advance throttle a tad to maintain, or reduce the descent rate. Now a final call, "Call sign", touch and go, full stop, low approach, a 500-foot low point before going around. A touch and go, is a landing, lower the nose, rolling, reach down and set the flaps at half flaps. (Remember that "blindfold" cockpit check from long ago? You just know where the lever is to set it.) Advance throttle to full power, check flap setting, a little back pressure on the stick and the plane will just lift off. By now one is near the end of the runway and a sweeping turn to downwind is appropriate. Make your downwind call.

Many feel they can master the plane. Perhaps only one class more senior at other training bases. Perhaps, 90 days to go. And now to enter a fun phase, formation flight, night flight, cross country, high speed low level and a really tough one Instrument qualification. Lots of talk about a next assignment.

One interesting thing about Randolph AFB. Lyndon Johnson was President and Air Force One would land there. Whenever he was coming in, all flying stopped. He'd come in about once a month and head up towards his ranch near Austin.

Our hanger was next to the snack bar. So, when he was coming in, some of us would wander over to the snack bar for a burger. Afterwards, we'd wander out and watch AF One land or taxi to parking. We'd hang on the fence. Usually a black car, with flags, would soon drive around a hanger and the President would get out. Always a Pol, he'd come over to the fence, along with two SS men, hand outstretched, "How are you boys doing?", and work the line, usually three or four of us. We were always upbeat. Never did get invited to the Ranch, however.

Formation flying was the most fun. Sort of like driving down the Interstate watching the car next to you. But rather than going 60 mph, you were going 600.

It is all relative. Two ship formations or four ship. We did all the acro maneuvers, loops, rolls, cloverleafs, whatever. Some times with an instructor, other times solo. Most everything done with hand signals, wing wiggles, or head nods. I was completely at ease. One rule: Keep up. Don't worry about the guy on your wing. I did make it a practice to set the engines at 96 percent, so others could keep up, otherwise, they'd have to crack an afterburner, and that would waste fuel.

Sometimes, we'd get in extended trail, about a thousand feet apart and traverse the skies. What was frowned upon, was going supersonic, which was easy to do. Point the nose down, and you'd get there fast. Four pounding supersonic "Booms" would get complaint calls to the base. Unconfirmed rumor has it that if done near Victoria, Texas, turkeys on the turkey farms would jump on each other and smother. As said, unconfirmed.

On the formation check ride, I did fine.

Something I have not mentioned: G Suits. Sort of like a lady's girdle device, that once on, squeezed the lower abdomen. And then leggings zipped up around each leg. The purpose is to squeeze blood up into the upper body half when putting the plane through its paces, and pulling multiple G forces. It sort of felt good, but a seven G's it was a hard squeeze.

The G suit was activated by air pressure from an engine. There was a large button to the pilot's seat left to check the hose connection and inflation, if desired. Wise not to carelessly put the heavy checklist to seat left, or you'll get a seven G squeeze on engine start.

Pilot training was not all happy events. We were scheduled to do low level, 350 knot, training. This was done at 300 feet off the ground. Navigation was visual, and on course points came up fast.

On this particular day, there was a low cloud deck, but clear below. Lt. Walt Vissers and his IP, Capt. Robert Gower, took off on their training mission. They headed Northwest, towards New Braunfels, where the ground was rolling hills, and grew higher. They were squeezed up towards the cloud deck. At some point, they hit the ground, skidded, and both pilots were killed. Another classmate gone.

My mission went fine and I "bombed" the little highway bridge on time. This navigation mission was a success, unlike my earlier Clemson experience.

Soon after, I had a night flight, my first. Major Turnbaugh and I flew up over Fort Worth, then turned right to Dallas. It was a wonderfully clear night in Texas, and the "Spiderweb" of colored lights was very impressive. After Dallas, we flew South over flying Houston. I was very surprised how dark and without lights flying over the Gulf actually was. Just a few oil wells. Then right turn back to base.

We had been practicing Instrument flight for some time. Now to get serious. For instrument training, the student gets in the rear cockpit, the IP in the front. Engines are started, taxi out to the runway. Simulated instrument flying is accomplished by drawing a canvass sheath overhead, essentially "Cocooning" the student in the rear cockpit.

The IP will taxi out and put the airplane on runway centerline. He will then tell you "Your airplane". With your feet on the brake bring the engines up to full throttle, check gauges, release brakes, throttles over center for afterburner. You are on your way. Just run the numbers, gear up, flaps up, climb to 1000 feet, left turn using 30 degrees of bank. Roll out, and then begin a climb at full throttle. The whole time you have been cross checking your instruments, as if you were in a fog bank. A quick call to departure and you are on your way to a training area.

Flying with Major Turnbaugh was enjoyable. While you were "In the Bag", generally sweating from effort, he would be up front telling you what a nice day it was or "we get paid to do this". Turnbaugh would work you based on your skills. "Turn left thirty degrees, climb to 33 thou, slow to 250 knots and gear down." Whatever, he felt you were capable of doing.

Instrument flying is a learned skill. It is achieved through an instrument gauge cross check, generally coming back to the principal instrument, the ADI. Or HSI. Attitude Directional Indicator and Horizontal Situation indicator. Sort of the "What's happening now" instruments and when combined with your altimeter, give a pilot a pretty good indication of their situation.

Think about looking at a clock. You do not stare at it. Rather you look and turn away and just know what time it is. So, it is with instrument flying.

Then you descend and make the different instrument approaches. Generally, you are told what to do by ground controllers. They need practice also to hone their skills. And after about an hour and a half, your IP will say I have the aircraft, and you push the "bag" back and he lands the airplane.

I personally preferred to fly in less than perfect weather, as it is realistic.

After landing you go back into the squadron room and go through a training sheet of what skills you have displayed, either satisfactorily or not. You need 100 percent satisfactory. Some learned easily, some took longer.

You reward was an Instrument Check Ride, the last hurdle. Now, if you don't demonstrate satisfactorily in a particular area, you are given more training, often in a flight simulator. Then a re-check in that area skill.

The Air Force is not going to give up on you now, having spent a half million dollars, making you a pilot. I made it through on the first check ride.

Congratulations, you are now an official Air Force Pilot, Class 68G, Randolph Air Force Base, Texas, with 232 flight hours.

We were told when we sat in the base theater that this would perhaps be the best year of our lives. I think it true.

Looking back to when we started, with about 90 young men in the theater, 27 graduated as pilots, with one killed., 28 total. We had a formal graduation ceremony, May 31st, 1968.

CHAPTER 3
MOVING OUT

I received my first set of orders. Nha Trang Airbase, Vietnam, Duty, Pilot AC-47.

I sold my 1964 Corvette Coupe to a Major at Randolph, a blue coupe, $1100 dollars. I wish I could have kept it.

I packed my bags, not really much, and sent some back to my parents' home. I think the Air Force did it for me.

I received TDY, "Temporary" duty orders to proceed to Survival School, Fairchild AFB, Spokane Washington. I had 5 days to get there, so I flew out after saying goodbye to my friends and pals. Off into the wild blue...

This survival school was to give you some idea of what to expect if you were shot down and captured. I of course realized it was a simulation, and reality would be much worse. School started a dusk on a Friday evening. Dress was military fatigues. We were to belly crawl under some wire for about 300 feet, upon which we were set upon and "captured". Much pushing and shoving, being yelled at and hands loosely tied behind our backs. A group of about ten were led off to a "Camp". Cloth bags were put over our heads.

Camp consisted of some half metal shells, gravel floors. We were to squat in there. Soon we were dragged out and put into individual box cells, no windows. "Prisoners" were expected to stand, our hands were untied. Loud music was played, along with moans and screams. A window in the door would slide open, and again more yelling. Every now and then, the door would suddenly open, no leaning. I decided to play a little, why not. So, I stood right up near the door, and when our "Guard" opened the door, I was right in his face. I think he was surprised, and gave me a push back, yelling.

The idea of all of this was to wear you out, fatigue. Morning finally came and we were marched out to a scrambled egg breakfast. That was more Air Force rules than anything. Some of us moved to "interrogation". Again, hooded movement. Others were put into small boxes, or holes in the ground with lids. We all got our chances to enjoy them.

In my interrogation, I was given an American flag, and told to burn it. I decided I would. The trainer pulled out a "Stop" flag, and explained to me that if I did that, I would be pictured in a propaganda video as an "Anti-American". I responded I figured the flags would have been hard to get, and burning was a proper disposal, giving them one less flag. Best was to treat it with loyalty. Flag away, he went back into his role. Lesson learned.

We were tired, dirty and hot. There were canteens of water for us. And again, the marching around with hoods, wear us down. Again, I decided to play. Every time I get a hood, or saw one, under my shirt it went. Then I would run it down to my metal shell and bury it under the stones. Do you know I created a shortage of hoods. The guards would look for some to use and had to go without.

At the end, I went and brought them back.

So, this went on all day and through the second night. Classroom propaganda sessions and yelling. They could not physically hurt us, so much realism was lost.

Sunday noon, the training was over. We thanked the trainers, all enlisted men, for their efforts. They asked us to individually evaluate the training, which I did in a one-on-one session. Interview completing, I told the trainer that I was the first in my flight class, and more would be coming. Would he want notes on them? Yes, and he got out his note pad. Name by name, I told him about as much as I could remember, and who might be getting a divorce, and maybe go a little easy in the personal area. Now one pal, Billy Spencer, had told me the name of his dog. He wrote that down. I heard later that Bill had thought his wife had been interviewed, and gave them that. It turned out that Bill Spencer was later shot down, captured, and spent nine months in North Vietnam prisons before being repatriated. I spoke with him on return via phone, and he said he was OK.

Busses took us back to quarters, to a wonderful shower, and later a good meal at the club. Since I had no further orders, and time, to take

Amtrak back to New Jersey, a very scenic trip. Upon arrival home, orders awaited me.

I was to proceed to England, AFB, Alexandria, LA, for a month of C-47 flight training. It was late July and hot in New Jersey and Louisiana. I got some ground school on the airplane, my check list and my manuals.

My primary flight instructor was a Lieutenant Colonel, close to retirement, whose name escapes me. He had a lot of C-47 flight experience. There were two student pilots on each flight. Our instructor mostly occupied the left, "command" seat, however a couple of times I get to be in the left seat, starting with the walk around inspection. Mostly it was right seat time.

I had to learn gear up and down, flap positioning, and fuel management. Then where the firing safety switch was located. All the flight instruments were "Old School" simplistic. The instrument panel itself was metal in this aircraft. I have flown in some that were wooden. Matters little.

Consider the AC-47 a flying gun platform. The guns are sticking out if empty windows on the left side. The theory was re-invented and proven in 1965. There are some stories about mail being delivered and picked up in a bucket in the "Wilds" somewhere. A bucket or basket was suspended on a long rope, and mail was to be placed in it, and pulled back up to the airplane. So, the story goes....

It is difficult to fly in a circle and keep your aim point on the same location. The aim point was defined by an old style (WWII) gun sight mounted on the left side pilots window sill. It had a dot in the center, and was called the "Pipper".

The pilot was to approach the target, which was to the left, in a manner that when the airplane as rolled into a 30-degree angled left turn the pipper moves to the target. Sounds easy, doesn't. The end result is you are flying the pipper dot.

The atmosphere is moving at five to ten miles an hour, with your aircraft flying in it. This means your circle is a series of constant corrections, while keeping the aircraft at a constant altitude. Think of nibbling around a cookie… at night.

Some of our activities took place at night, using the light from parachute flares that we would drop. When we were on a flare only mission, we would fly a half circle, then a race track 30 second line, and reverse course with another half circle. Ideally, that would be done in a manner that would give you a two-minute lap, as that was the burn time of the flare. Then you make adjustments due to winds.

All is much easier in the day light, which most of our training took place. The trainees would swap into the left seat when it was their turn. We would fly about a four-hour mission, and then go back and analyze our efforts. It looks easy on paper.

At England AFB, we flew about ten sessions, with maybe 20 hours of "stick" time. It was more of familiarization with the aircraft and procedures. There were no old-time pilots in our classes, all Second Lieutenants out of flight school.

One mission was of interest. The one and only time we would fire all three guns at fast fire, 6000 rounds a minute, in all of my training. And since we only carried 18,000 rounds, it would have been a real "quickie" use up. There was a large pond with a pole in the center. The IP rolled the pipper in on the pole, squeezed the trigger, which was located in the right side of the control wheel. The water literally exploded from the bullets. The co-pilot could see it through the pilot's window, and the other student standing in the aisle looking out the window. Gunners in the back could look out the absent cargo door. It was only a five second burst. Long bursts were wasteful.

The reaction force from the firing pushed the tail around, effectively moving the impact point. This was just a demo, and an only time exercise. In Vietnam, on one mission, and the only one, we fired two guns for ten seconds, as a show of force display to break up a "Troops in Contact" firefight.

My miserable TDY to Alexandria, LA, was over. I was there about a month, the hottest most humid month. A taste of Vietnam. I stayed in a Holiday Inn, and evenings went to listen to the same band playing the same show every night. The one nice break was a girl friend from my San

Antonio pilot training time came over for a long weekend and we went to New Orleans. Liked the shrimp, not the donuts.

Meanwhile, I received another set of TDY orders. This was better. I was to go to Homestead AFB, Miami. Florida, for water survival training. A good deal.

After some initial Instruction on water survival, I was transported to the dock in Biscayne Bay, and taken out on a flat-topped boat. I was issued over water survival gear, which was attached to the seat area of my parachute harness, and an already opened parachute draped behind me. A strap, with a quick release, was attached to the front of the harness. The other end of the strap was attached to an idling powerful speed boat out in front of boat.

A couple of guys held the strap and told me to lean back as the speed boat took up line slack. I had a good idea about what was next as I had done this in parachute training on dry ground at Randolph. I was to take steps when they released the strap and signaled the speed boat. I did and was airborne heading up several hundred feet. At that point I was to release one side of the water survival gear so it would hang down. The speed boat allowed the strap to go limp and that was my signal to actuate the quick release, allowing the tow strap to fall away.

I floated down, enjoying the view. Splash! Into the warm water of Biscayne Bay, pulled my inflated life raft to me and enjoyed a leisure half hour float. That was it. Headed back home the next day.

After a couple of days, I received more orders. I was to travel from Newark Airport, NJ, to Clark Air Base, Philippines. I would be going to Jungle Survival School. There was also two weeks of leave time before departure, that would put me into early September, 1968. Borrowing my folk's car, a really neat 1964 Pontiac LeMans, I went and visited a number of my friends. There was a lot of discussion about their draft number. My college pal from across the street, Steve Petrucione, had joined the Peace Corps, and was off to where ever. It was hard being in the town where my old girlfriend lived. Lots of memories.

Leave passed quickly, and I sorted through my clothes. A few civilian outfits, shoes, bathing suit, and underwear. The rest was a couple of flight suits and fatigues. I didn't need much. I did manage to fill a trunk and an Air Force Issue bag.

My brother had left for college, and the day came to head for Newark Airport and the rest of the story.

CHAPTER 4
LEAVING THE STATES

I found my seat on the plane. An aisle seat just aft of the wing. My trunk and Air Force bag were in the hold, and ticketed through to Clark AFB, Philippines. This was going to be a long day and night set of flights. It was early September. Somewhat wistful, I put my seat back, and tried to close my eyes. About 40 minutes into the flight, again a Braniff, the stewardesses pushed a cart down the aisle, and starting from the rear, moved forward. I realized I recognized one of the stewardesses. We greeted each other as she moved the cart by.

The flight was to be about six hours to San Francisco. Once things had settled down, I went to the back and talked with her in empty seats cross aisle. That helped to pass the time. She had to get up when the call light went on, or she served a lunch. She wished me well on the remainder of my trip. Little was spoken about Viet Nam.

There were a couple of hours dwell time in San Francisco. Not much to do. Again, a coach seat for the long leg, about 10 hours, on Braniff, with a new crew. We flew through the night, landing and disembarking in the morning. My orders only took me as far as Clark AFB, where I was to attend "Jungle Survival Training".

I found the Air Force transportation office and somehow my bag and trunk appeared. I got on a "Short Bus" and was taken to the housing office. It was getting hot and humid. I could feel it through my shoes. There I was given a BOQ assignment and somehow found my way. Trunk and bag were delivered, and I was pleased to be in the air conditioning.

Since my body timing was off, I got hungry in the early afternoon. Stepping out I realized it was raining, a nice steady downpour. No thunder, just rain. I had a map inside and found the Officers Club was not far away. The rain had let up, and avoiding the puddles, found the "O" Club. It was typical of the Pacific, lots of dark wood, not much going on. I looked over the dinner menu and ordered something. Paid in US dollars. Went out and raining again, hustled over to quarters.

One of the things I learned in the PI, (Philippines) try to find plants with large leaves to stand under. I wondered if Viet Nam would be like this.

I finally found my way to the training center and "Jungle Survival". Mostly Air Force folks, 50/50 Officers and enlisted.

Some of the classes were interesting. Some like what to do with your parachute and use of a jungle penetrator. Now a jungle penetrator is a device lowered from a hovering helicopter on a cable. Let it ground out, then lower to horizontal two of the three legs, straddle the penetrator and sit on the legs, Wrap the retaining strap around you and clip it. One arm around the penetrator and give a thumbs up signal. Wrap the other arm around, and put your head up against it.

The cable is supposed to lift you, and as long as you don't get shot as you dangled, crewmen will pull you onto the helicopter. Hold on for dear life and the crew men will uncover your arms and free the penetrator. Until then you are not rescued.

You learn about other neat things that you can find in your survival vest, like a little hand-held signal rocket and your emergency radio, about the size of a brick.

Now some of the rules such as "Eat what the monkey's eat", or if eating greens, hold them in your mouth for two minutes before chewing to make sure there are no reactions. And finally, you can eat any ocean fish raw that looks like a fish, except Atlantic Red Snapper. Why it is I don't know. I am reminded of that training as I eat sushi later in life.

Our training also included an overnight exercise in hiding from anyone looking for you. Again, in our fatigues, we were led to an area, had a little supper and told to hide away. There were Filipino guides who would try to search us out, and would be rewarded if they found us.

I went out away, found the nastiest vegetation area and curled up. A couple of hours later my skin felt creepy, and taking my flashlight, and risking exposure, looked at my calf. There were tinny little red mites walking about. I decided to let them be, and slept. By dawns light I got up and found my way back. There was some scrambled eggs and coffee.

I never did discern if the guides even went out to look for us. A bus picked us up and back to Clark I went. I took a shower and a nap in the air conditioning. And no bug bites.

I hung out for a couple of days. I even met a local gal at the Club. Turned out she was Catholic and of Spanish heritage, as the PI's were under Spain until we took over in 1900. Tried some local seafood. It was OK

After a couple of days, having read all the on-hand magazines, wondered where my next orders were. I also wondered if this time counted towards my year in Viet Nam duty. Plus, I was tired of all the rain.

I finally went by Personnel and inquired, thinking they might ask "Where have you been?". But no, soon orders where put in my hand, travel to Nha Trang, RVN, 3rd SOS.

And to once again travel commercially, one received a page of orders, which was handed to an airline ticket representative and receive back a boarding pass. Once again Braniff, and destination Saigon, Tan Son Nhut AFB. Nine AM departure.

I arranged for transport to the airline departure in the AM. In the morning I left and once again my bag and trunk followed, and were absorbed by the baggage area at the civilian field. The airplane left on time, and totally filled with GI's some new, some returning from R&R week long leaves. I had a window seat and just rested or looked out as we descended. After a couple of hours, we have descended and were flying over the low lands. I was looking out, fully expecting to see some evidence of combat, and wondering if anybody was shooting at us.

We soon landed and parked in the civilian area. I went down to the concrete on some roll up stairs, and found my trunk and bag. I really didn't know where to go next, or who to ask, but a number of Vietnamese men approached to take our bags. I didn't know how to pay him, but had my wallet out, and he indicated by pointing at the dollar bills. I gave him three and pointed at my bag and trunk. He picked up my bag and grabbing my trunk end handle, begin at drag it off, with me following.

There was a smell about Vietnam, hard to describe, I guess tropical. And hot, as I was glad to finally reach some shade of military buildings. My baggage man took me to a military transport area, pointed to the desks and left. I went up and asked about transport to Nha Trang. I produced some order set and he said I could get a flight about noon. Where? Here, just be here. I waited, and bout noon a flight to Nha Trang was called out. This time it was an Air Force C-130, and somehow dragging my gear I got on and found seat, a pulled down canvas seat. It was hot.

Engines started, the ramp was pulled up, and we taxied out and took off. There was no air conditioning until well airborne, and little of it. This was my second flight on a C-130, the first being at ROTC summer camp, where most on board threw up.

We flew up the coast and about an hour later landed. Somehow, I got my gear to the housing office and got a BOQ assignment. I checked in and it was totally different. I don't think it was air conditioned. There was screen from about six feet to the roof line. And the smell and sound of war were here. It seems there was a Korean encampment adjoining the Air Base, and they regularly shot howitzers up into the hills. Every few minutes there was a boom.

So here I was bedraggled, and I found the "O" club and had a meal served by Vietnamese waitresses. And a canned cool drink, no ice. Nothing fancy. Dusk was approaching. It was a Friday evening, my first day in country. I went back to my "Q" undressed and headed for the showers. But first some "Can" time in the open stalls. I wondered what kind of toilet paper they had, Rough Military? I listened to the continuous booms of cannon shots.

As I sat, I heard a different sound, "Wrack", and noted that it was different. And another, that was followed by the sound of s siren, and voices of men as they clamored into the latrine. Most were hitting the floor, and I dove for it also. The third "Wrack", hit right outside of the "Q", and threw dirt through the screen onto me, now stretched out. I began thinking this was not as easy as I thought it would be. First night in Vietnam and almost hit by what were mortars. One more Wrack, and soon the siren stopped.

Men got up and left muttering amongst themselves. It seems the latrines were built with concrete walls for the first few feet, thustly considered a shelter area. I went and took a warm shower wondering about all of this. I did manage to sleep.

Saturday, I just hung out looking about and listening. I went over to the nearby club for some lunch. Afterwards went back to the bar where a scene surprised me. There was a TV on a table against the back wall. Gathered around it, perhaps 12 to 15 Army guys, watching intently. What were they watching? The B&W TV show "Combat" about fighting in Europe in WWII. Combat! Of all things, a bunch of Army Officer Grunts, who only needed to step out the door to be in the real thing. They were all dressed in their fatigue uniforms. Strange going on.

I hoped to find something to read. Nothing, quite bored. Just hung out and had an early dinner. I wanted to move on.

Sunday, slept in some, ending at the club. I was lounging at the bar, when a fellow I had met at survival school walked in. We greeted and began talking, I told him about my Friday evening experience. "Well, what did it sound like?" WRACK!

"Just like that!" and I hit the floor. Soon the siren sounded, followed by another WRACK. The TV Grunts hit the floor also. My pal got down also. I felt like the combat vet on Sunday, after Friday's event.

Soon it was over. Dusting off, there was some talk about a Jeep out front. We went out and looked, it had taken a direct hit and was somewhat broken up. I later learned the first one had hit an airman's unoccupied bunk in a nearby enlisted dorm. Maybe bracketing us at the club? That was my Sunday.

Monday, I found 3rd SOS and 4th SOS Admin and presented my orders. After some shuffling, orders were produced assigning me to the 3rd Special Operations Squadron at Bien Hoa. Where was it? Down near Saigon. Drill here, drill there, hurry up and wait. I really don't remember how I got to Bien Hoa, along with my gear. Mid-afternoon I walked into the "Spooky" air-conditioned dorm, down the hallway to the center lounge area. I introduced myself to a Major and said I was assigned here. His response, "Good let's find you a room". And he ushered me into the first dorm style room on the left. The lower bunk was unoccupied.

Later, a Nav Captain said, "Hey whose stuff is in my room?" I introduced myself, and said it was mine. He did not look happy, but so what. A Captain Nav and a 2nd Lt Pilot.

I looked around and found the showers and latrine. Double ended room doors, no doors on the stalls. At the right-hand end was a white wallboard, and four designations" Spooky 71 through Spooky 74. Then some names, and across the top I figured dates, 1 to 31. There were three names associated with each Spooky, and "x's" in the date blocks. I quickly learned that this was the daily fling schedule. I knew none of the names or their positions.

There were some towels on the bed, and I decided a shower was in order. After showering, I put on some civilian clothes and went back out into the center lounge and introduced myself. Perhaps ten new names, some younger, some older. Dressed in all manner from fatigues to flight suits. A couple got up and left, I guessed to go fly. I asked about dinner around here, and the reply was "We are going to the club, want to join us?" "Sure", was my reply.

I asked questions and learned where the chow hall was located, the Post Office and the theater. All in walking distance. What about supply? Probably a Jeep ride. Oh, OK.

There was some beer in the fridge and I was offered one, which I accepted. I felt a little out of sorts as I was the only one dressed as a civilian. I guess I could have changed into a flight suit and black boots. Soon, the word "Ready? "Was offered and we walked out into the five PM heat to a Jeep. "You drive", I was told, as the FNG's always drove. "FNG" as you might guess stood for "F...g New Guy".

I got in and looked about. A floor stick, clutch pedal, truck steering wheel. I don't remember if there was a key, I don't think so. Left dash, a pointer knob, "Off, On and Start". Four others got in, three in back one "Shotgun". Depressing the clutch pedal, I slowly turned the knob to "Start", and it did. Released it ran. I moved the shifter left and back, a good choice. A little gas, and a slow lift of the clutch pedal. We were off, the fellow in the left seat indicated turn around, and soon we reached to road and made a right turn. Out of the corner of my eye, I noticed three large gun barrels sticking up across the street. They were 155mm, I would learn later.

We drove around the perimeter road, the breeze felt good. Bien Hoa City, with a large water tower were on my left as I drove. With a couple of turns we reached the "O" Club, and I felt good that I had not bucked anyone out. In fact, I was pretty smooth, I guess from my Corvette experience. In we went.

Another dark club and soon found a table. Beer in bottles all around. The waitress was Vietnamese. I had been warned about the water and Ice, so stayed clear, watching others. No salads, fruit or uncooked food. "Eat what the monkey's eat" came to mind. I think I had a hamburger and fries. American staple.

We finished up, and soon left. It was still light enough to make my way back to the hooch. My first day in Bien Hoa.

CHAPTER 5
LEARNING THE ROPES-BIEN HOA

I was here. I had my USA gear, Flight Suit, black leather boots. I needed to get to supply and draw my Viet Nam gear. I hitched a ride over to Operations, a three-building compound. I rode over across the ramp, by the Spooky's parked in their revetments and got out in front of what I was to know as Operations. It was a large trailer, one center door and one left end door. A couple of steps up and in.

There was a Major seated at a desk, and introducing myself, I presented some orders. It was obvious I was an FNG, a lost soul. I figured out he was the Operations Officer. Seemed like a nice enough fellow. He told me I'd be assigned to Lt. Colonel Hyde's crew as co-pilot, although he referred to him as "Colonel Hyde".

Apparently, Hyde was listening in his back office, and he came out to say hello. He was about 5'9", graying, with a thin moustache, Command Pilot wings. He said we would be flying together in a couple of days. "Ok, Thanks" and he turned and went back into his office.

I remarked I needed to get to Supply and get my Vietnam gear. "We'll get somebody to take you by there." There was another officer nearby, and he asked him to take me over to Supply. We soon left and in a matter of minutes, we were at Supply. We both got out of the Jeep and went in.

A sergeant appeared at the window and I told him I needed to draw my gear. I told him I was going to be a "Spooky", and he could see my USA flight suit. Somehow, he ascertained my size, and four new flight suits were stacked in the window. "Boot size?", "Look on the bottom of your boot", which I did and ascertained it was a size 10. He had a list under some plexiglass and began going down it. "Wrist Watch? yes. I still had my chrome US watch, but might as well get issue. I then got a mesh survival vest and a gun holster. The supply sergeant produced a form, checked off some blocks, turned it and said "sign here".

I picked up my stack of clothing, shoes and gear, and back to the jeep. Can we go back to the "hooch?" Sure. Along the way I remarked that "You All" had your rank and wings in black thread. Where is that done? "Over next to the BX, at the cleaners". Can we go there, "Sure". "Oh, I only have US dollars, where do I get the script used here?" Finance was the reply. "Can we go there". "OK". I could sense I was using him up.

I want into Finance and exchanged my dollars for script of various face values. I was given a form to fill out where to send my pay and other options like next of kin. "I'll bring this back." I really didn't know how to complete it.

I inquired about lunch. "Next to the BX" and he agreed he wanted something.

We parked and I saw the cleaners. My driver pal tilted my seat forward and told me to put my stuff under it. He stayed with the jeep. I grabbed the new uniforms, and went in. A Vietnamese lady was behind the counter. I pointed to my flight suit and said I needed them "Embroidered" pointing at my name and rank. "One Bar", holding up one finger. She obviously had done this before. "Name?" Slocum, pointing at mine. Nodding, she gave me a slip of paper, a ticket. "You come back, two days." Very authoritative.

Now the flight suits were a little different. Patches were no longer sewn on. What was sewn on was fuzzy Velcro, the pattern matching the patch. Then on the patches, and name tag was put the Velcro hooks. A little conceal of information. I have heard some had nickname nametags made up. Never saw any. Probably Navy guys.

I went out, and went to a burger bar. I ordered, along with a Coke, a canned coke, and fries. I think it was two dollars script. She said something and soon a wrapped burger appeared, along with fries. I managed to find some ketchup. And we sat at a table outside and made small talk, all the while keeping eyes on the Jeep. Leaving, I saw a barber shop next door. Good to know. A lot of GI's in and out of the BX.

I decided that I was going to grow a mustache since I would not be wearing an oxygen mask.

The next few days were a whirlwind. I can't remember anything other than learning a few names and faces. I seemed to be the only new guy.

Never did see Col. Hyde in the lounge area. Limited TV channels. Guys mostly read or played cards.

Soon my name appeared on the board, Spooky 71 with Hyde. I watched in the afternoons as others gathered up and left. I had gotten my fresh flight suits and was breaking in my comfortable mesh "jungle" boots. I just followed a crowd out and got in a "Bread" truck, off to the flight line.

The Spooky operations consisted of three buildings. The Operations trailer, which I had been in, across the road, which turned out to be a taxiway, another smaller trailer and a pitch roof building. The smaller trailer was a crew rest trailer, with bunks. Crews flying the second launches could go there and rest. It was air conditioned.

Walking through a screened door and area, and walking to the rear was an area lined with lockers. "Find an open locker, without "Stuff" in it. Most had combination locks on the handles, signifying some claim. We were supposed to keep things in there after flights, or personal things when flying. I left my wallet after removing my ID. I learned later to just leave my wallet back at the hooch. I later got a little "mini" wallet for my ID and a couple of script dollars, which I carried.

Dog tags on, taped together, my survival vest, headset, and holster, I went out front where there were some chairs, and sat down. Soon began a pre-flight briefing. Operations gave a weather report for the area, standard I guessed, just hot. Then a captain in fatigues, not a Spooky member, got up and talked about Intel in the area and what to expect. None seemed very interested. I guess old news. Then, we went to a room nearby, with Dutch doors. Weapons storage. Others gave their names. I said I was a new guy, and the clerk looked about, and handed me a revolver and six rounds. I indicated my holster bullet loops were empty, and asked for six more. He sort of looked at me, like "Stupid", and gave me six more bullets. He pulled out a form, looked at my name and wrote it down. Taking the gun back, he logged the serial number down. He had opened the revolver chambers, and I was to load it with the barrel pointed in this can, which I did. Pistol to holster, I walked out front. I sort of felt like an old-time gunslinger. I followed Hyde to the bread truck. Most carried their pistols. A couple of enlisted men had rifles, AR15's. All the crews did their pre-flights now while light, just to get them done. Once we got to the plane, I noticed a few maintenance fellows about, along with a start power unit.

I stood near the cargo door opening, and said hello to the crew members as they walked up. All were experienced, and the enlisted men knew each other. Seven crew men. And one additional, a Vietnamese member joined us. Eight total. He did not say anything.

Somehow Hyde indicated, time to go. I climbed three steps up a short, attached ladder, and skirted along the lashed down ammo cans, walking up the sloped floor to the cockpit area. I put my opened checklist on the dash cowl. Hyde was doing the walk around.

I looked over the cockpit, sort of wondering what to do next. I pushed the prop handles up, throttles back and looked at the mixture knobs. I looked at the radios, and the knobs looked to be in number one channel. I looked at my seat, moved the lap belts, and noted the bullet proof vest, compacted on the seat.

Now the rule was you did not wear your vest, but rather sat on it. I had my survival vest on, and I'm not sure if I was to wear it, what went on first. And the theory was that any bullet destined for you would not come in from front or back, but up through the floor. Therefore, sit on it.

I sat down, and Hyde appeared on the doorway, and moved into his seat. A couple of quick adjustments, and he put on his seat belt and shoulder straps, while I clumsily did the same. "Ready?", looking at me, while I had my check list in hand "Starting engines".

He indicated out the window, and the Auxiliary Power Unit (APU) power churred into life. A quick "Clear" and he reached up and initiated the starter switch, number one engine, while reaching over and moving the mixture knob from off to rich, then his hand back to the throttle lever, moving it forward. The engine caught and jumped into life, and he quickly set throttle about 1000 RPM. He looked over at me, and I looked out my open window, and holding op two fingers, moved them. I looked on the prop area and said "Clear". With that he started number two engine. All very efficiently, as the AGE cable was pulled and the unit pulled away.

Hyde had his headset on, right ear exposed, and put mine on, left ear exposed for cross cabin communication. A maintenance man out front, waved us to pull out.

Not really knowing what to do, I pressed the button on my headset cable and said "Bien Hoa, Spooky 71, taxi, takeoff", back came "Roger, Spooky". Nothing was said to me.

Now to turn the plane, I had to release the tail wheel lock, allowing the tail wheel to swivel, which I did, and Hyde, using differential brakes, turned the plane on the ramp. We did two more turns to get to the parallel taxiway and the runup area at the end of the runway. I guess I was doing OK so far.

We reached the end of the runway and run up area, and again I released the tailwheel as Hyde turned the plane towards the runway. Parked, he held the brakes, as I nervously ran my finger down the "Starting Engines" check list and flipped over to the "Before Take Off" list.

Hyde advanced the throttles to 30 inches of boost. Selecting engine one, he turned the magneto selection knob from "Both", to number two mag and checked for rpm drop, then back to both, followed by turning to one magneto and looking for the same, then back to both. Finally, he pulled the number one throttle back to idle, and the mag selector to off, and back again to both, when the engine indicated it would shut off, if desired. Then throttle to 30 inches and did the same with engine two.

Once completed, he reached over and pulled the prop setting full back as the props pulled down, cycling the prop pitch. This he did twice, returning the throttles to the 1000 RPM position. Obviously, a veteran pilot. Hyde looked about, and then over his right shoulder to ensure the back-end crew were seated. Final item "Flaps Set" take off position. No flaps were the standard take off setting.

I looked at the "Take Off" checklist and said "Boost Pumps –On" indicating the fuel boost pumps were on for takeoff, and reaching down to release the tail wheel. We turned and taxied forward. I looked up at the final approach glide path and out of habit, said "Final is Clear". We turned and lined up with runway centerline. I released the tail wheel, "Tail Wheel –Locked" I don't remember making a take off call, but both of us reached up and turned the radio knob to position two, Tower.

Hyde advanced power to about 46 inches of boost, then moved the throttle levers in small increments to 48 inches. All looked good, and we moved down the runway. I reached over and guarded the throttles, at 48 inches. Soon the tail came up, and I saw 70, then 80 knots, the plane lightened and lifted off, as we climbed at about 120 knots. Hyde brought the power back to climb power, maintaining 120 knots.

Soon Hyde said, "Gear Up", and I reached down and opened the valve raising the gear. Once indicating up. I closed the valve position. A quick check indicated 800 pounds hydraulic pressure, all good.

A relievedly clear night, we headed for Saigon Combat Air Patrol "CAP", leveling at 3000 foot altitude. I had really no idea what we were doing. Hyde switched his radio to the airborne control frequency. I did mine the same. In a few moments the Nav, who had been quiet, called out on his radio to "Hillsboro" control that we were entering the area, and they acknowledged.

With the lights of Saigon off to our left, Hyde indicated we were going to be flying a box pattern in this area, with three-to-five-minute legs. A circuit could be 12 to 20 minutes. He then reached out and set the mixtures to auto lean. Leaving the boost pumps on, he said, lets run out of the aft tanks. I carefully switched the fuel feed to the aft tanks, boost pumps off, and tank fuel level knob position to right rear. Tanks full, 200 gallons.

Hyde then said we'll fly each an hour, then switch. He indicated that I should now take over, and settled back. I'm sure he watched initially as I flew, trying to find a pattern. I'd reach over and move the elevator trim wheel, trying to find the "Just Right" wheel feel. At least I thought so. I got to like about 25-degree bank angle in each of the four turns, with enough back pressure to hold altitude. My hour was soon up, and Hyde took over. He moved the mixture controls to "Auto Rich" indicating he was "De-Coking" the engines from running at a constant speed for an hour, to eliminate carbon buildup. After two minutes he returned the mixtures to "Auto-Lean." It was standard procedure.

We took off around 7PM, and planned to return, if no action, leaving the CAP around 11:30PM, landing at midnight. I'd get three hours of control time, each night. About five hours of seat time. The schedule was four days on, three off. I'd get about twelve hours a week, 48 a month. But no take offs or landings. Maybe a hundred hours a month of seat time.

Since we checked in and took off before dinner, we could draw an inflight meal. Somehow, they arrived before we completed our briefing, and we could pick them up as we left. I regularly preordered fried chicken. It had three pieces of chicken, a roll, a fruit and a water. I usually ate after I flew my first hour. Can't remember Col. Hyde, having a dinner, but I'm sure he did.

October 1968, was just a "Fly Cap" month. Nothing happening. November started the rainy season, the "Monsoon". The VC didn't like the rain, and month either. The C-47 was an old plane, and all the seals had long before dried up. Flying in the rain meant rain water dripping into the cockpit. I soon went by supply and drew a poncho, which I would wear. I again would wear it in the second half of my tour when flying through storms along the Mekong when flying out of Laos into Thailand. But that is another story.

I also found a canvas bag, to put my "Stuff" into, and used it on my way to and from the plane. I guess I was sort of becoming an experienced flight veteran. But no action.

One night, we did get called off cap and told to proceed northwest to the Old Michelin Plantation, where some tanks had gotten stuck in the monsoon mud. It ended up being a flare only mission, to provide light so that the VC would not be encouraged to molest the tanks. The tanks were the new lightweight tanks. Our flares lasted about an hour and a half, and we gave control fair warning, so another Spooky could be launched to take over. I was surprised we didn't land and reload, ready to go back out. Light was provided until morning.

Christmas and the holidays meant little. I think we had Turkey on Christmas at the Club. The regular enlisted mess, I expect, had turkey also. We drew Cap on New Year's Eve. We did not know what to expect, and exercising good judgement Hyde climbed to 10,000 feet at midnight to fly our cap. It was wise, because at midnight, all sorts of tracer rounds opened up, arcing about the sky. We were above it all on a clear night. A million-dollar display.

January came and our troubles began. We, and everybody else, received a bad lot of flares. The flares would not ignite, leaving the GIs on the ground in darkness. February Vietnamese New Year, TET, was coming and there was beginning to be a lot of movement. The 1968 Tet was bad for the USA, as we were almost knocked out by the surprise attacks. We were on our toes this year.

To remedy the situation, we were throwing two flares at a time, hoping for at least one to ignite. But this gave us only about 45 minutes of support.

I want to describe a somewhat related incident. I don't know who I was flying with, as Lt. Col. Hyde, had rotated back to the USA, without even a goodbye message to the Squadron. The new Squadron Commander was Lt. Col Davidson. I was a floating asset, experienced, and plugged in as necessary.

On this particular evening, we were pulled off of first cap to support US troops who were dug in and being probed by the VC. The GI's requested illumination support. We located them and began dropping flares, two at a time, and sometimes getting one light, others two. On one particular loop, we dropped two and there was total darkness. We got ground complaints, and were doing the best we could to come around. Suddenly there were tracer rounds flying about on the ground, and yelling over the radio, which we could hear. We thought the VC had suddenly attacked in the darkness.

We asked what was going on, thinking we would be called on to use our guns. The reply was "A Tiger!" Followed by "a tiger grabbed a GI by the shoulder and tried to pull him out of his hole!". Whaaa... In the darkness, a tiger snuck in and grabbed the man. Thus, the uproar.

I guess the tiger had gotten used to an easy meal, VC body parts, etc., and made a move. Imagine the letter home... "Dear Mr. and Mrs. we regret to inform you..."

We were able to give them light until we ran out. The Army had illumination howitzer rounds and they had to use them until the next

Spooky could get on the scene. Never did like flying around Army fired rounds.

CHAPTER 6
HOOCH LIFE

I arrived at Bien Hoa Airbase in September 1968, after a bag drag from Clark AB in the PI, by Braniff, and them by military support flights to Nha Trang AB, and finally Bien Hoa, now my home base. Bien Hoa is an older fighter TAC base, single runway, adjoining the huge Long Binh Army supply base. Bien Hoa is north northeast, about 30 road miles, from Saigon.

The quarters were single story, dormitory style, 12 rooms to a leg, split by a lounge area on one side and showers and toilets opposing. Two legs, each room with two men, bunk beds. The building was air conditioned, vinyl floor tiles. Exterior walls in the lounge area were concrete to about five feet, offering some protection. The lounge, connected by hallways, had one exit door. Dorm rooms each had a window, venetian blinds, overhead florescent lighting.

When I arrived it was afternoon, and there were a few others in the lounge area. I was shown a room occupied with one other near the lounge area. I dropped my gear and settled in, trying to fit in.

Trying to describe the lifestyle, I would say the diverse personalities were much like the later movie and TV show, Mash. But ours were all officers housed here. The enlisted men were elsewhere. The group was diverse with young lieutenants, sprinkled with captains, majors and senior Lt. Colonels, all pilots or navigators. Vietnam was different, with someone always coming or going due to 12-month duty tours. There were FNG's (F.. New Guys) to fellows with short ribbons. I don't think we had any Academy officers. The senior officers had been holding desk jobs, while lieutenants were fresh out of flight school. Captains and majors had principally flight duties, mostly MAC cargo.

But Spooky aircrews were unique, they flew only at night. Their day started around 4PM, showering, dressing, and those flying, heading to operations around 5:30PM. They would return around 6AM. A few stayed, while others went to the mess hall for breakfast, then back to the hooch, and turned in for a day of sleep.

Crewmembers not flying might go to the club for dinner. Some got together and went to dinner at a Chinese restaurant at Long Binh. Then they stayed up most of the night, reading, writing and playing cards. A few would sip cocktails and chat.

This was the pattern for every day. The only difference was the rotation of the crews. On non-flying days, some would make a BX run or get a haircut. Letters home were important along with Post Office checks. Each of us had a PO box assigned at the nearby Post Office. No need for stamps, at least for letters, because mail from the combat zone was free, with the word "Free" replacing the stamp. Incoming mail went to a designated "APO", Army/Air Force Post Office, and routed to Bien Hoa.

JUNG AND VE

I can't say enough about Jung and Ve, our hooch housekeepers. Jung was originally from North Vietnam, where her father was a government official. When the French were pushed out, the family moved South. Jung was educated and spoke and understood several languages.

Ve was the wife of a Vietnamese paratrooper. She was considerably taller than Jung, who was barely five feet tall. The two worked well together. Jung was not married.

Jung and Ve took care of everything. Our quarters were spotless, our bed linens changed regularly, our clothing washed and folded, or closet hung. She knew what belonged to whom, and took pride in their work. Jung, in all serious talk told me that someone, a year before, had stolen a shirt from her clothes line and she was looking for him. I "CaCa Dow" (phonetically), stating she would cut his head off. She meant it.

From time to time, she would pull out the electric skillet and cook us a very nice Vietnamese meal. Always delicious.

I would always tease Ve to leave her husband and be with me. She pretended to not understand English, but one day, I awoke while she was cleaning my room, desk. I said, "Ve, what time is it?" and she replied in beautiful clipped British accent English "It is three-thirty" and laughed. She never said another word to me in English, but I knew she knew more than she put on.

Example of Jung's care. There were Vietnamese workers doing a cleaning and polishing of the floors. All of us were to go to a mandatory "Commanders Call" in the base theater while this was taking place. The Commander was to cover numerous admin requirements. The real objective was to get us out of the building so the work could be done.

Upon returning around five PM, someone said "I've been robbed, all my valuables are gone". And sure enough, from every room, if anything had been there, like a civilian watch or ring, it was gone. Most all the guys went to their rooms. Soon after, someone said, "Check your pillowcases", and sure enough, there was each mans "stuff". Jung knew what was of value, and had secreted it into our pillowcases, and remade our beds.

One more story. The Vietnamese "Tet", 1969 New Year, was soon approaching. There were reports of considerable growing activity. It seemed that in town, the VC would drink and brag about upcoming events. There was always talk among us that we would soon see more action. One afternoon, Jung came up to me and said "If you see a man with a red handkerchief in his shirt pocket, he is VC, you shoot him right away". That was their signal. I passed it on to Intel.

I should by now advise that I had grown a fine handlebar moustache. It took three months. I'm now getting back into playing bridge in the evenings. Oh, let's see, we have two TV channels, a B&W TV. Some guys watch Combat, Bonanza, and a new show Star Trek.

With the 12-month tours, guys come and go. I want to relate something that was always interesting. I may have mentioned earlier that there was three Army 155mm cannons nearby. They were down the hall, out the door and across the street. Then there was a road, a grass berm and a wire fence. It was maybe 300 feet away.

There was always a mix of guys in the lounge. Around Christmas, the guys decided to build a bar. With a little help from the Civil Engineering group, bricks and concrete were scrounged, along with a little help. It seemed to go up in a day. Someone in our squadron scrounged from the army a used helicopter blade. It was easily shortened by a hacksaw, and a little help. And even though it was tapered, it became the bar top. I never saw a drink slip off.

Saturday was just another day for us. There were two or three tables usually occupied, three or four folks at the bar. Well, every Saturday night, the cannons were rotated to point over our hooch. And at two AM, all three were fired simultaneously. You can only imagine the roar and concussion. The new guys would throw their drinks and have a look of absolute panic. The old-timers would just look at their watches. I called it the "Two O'clock Whistle". It was never discussed beforehand, so the "Newbies" never had a chance.

The firing was a planned event, an H&I, Harassment and Interdiction, exercise. I don't know where the rounds landed.

There was one event of mention. It seemed that three at the tables one particular night, months earlier, found themselves over served. Self-indulged. They decided they wanted to shoot the guns. Well, an hour after midnight, on a particular Saturday, they went across the street and began yelling to the Army guys. There was finally a response, and they stated their desires. The Army guys joked back and began rotating the guns. Be it known; it was about 2AM anyway. Our guys exclaimed they wanted to tell them to fire. The Army guys strung them along, telling them they were loading. Finally, the hour approached and the Army guys asked if they were ready? With the remainder of their drinks in hand, they responded. I was not there, but I believe there was some countdown implied. And seconds after the yell of "Fire" erupted, the 2AM cannons went off.

The men were knocked to the ground by the concussions, and since they were not wearing ear protection, lost their hearing for days. Luckily, they in their stupor retained their ear drums. But notice was given that such forays were forbidden.

I want to relate an incident that makes me smile to this day. In March, we got a new Squadron Commander, LTC John Rowe. It was his first command. Personality-wise, think of Mash's Henry Blake. Col Rowe was from Ohio.

He arrived one bright and sunny afternoon, dragging his duffle bag. He entered the hooch, and blinking, tried to get his eyes used to the shadowed hallway lighting. There was a lot of yelling going on, and in his recovered vision there were four naked men standing in the hallway. One was on a headlock, one with their back to him, the other two facing. The yelling was "I'm going to stick it right up your ass", and as Col Rowe tells the story it was "This is my first command, and I have to deal with this…" "What have I gotten myself into?" The men who were all great friends, and shall remain nameless for now, soon broke up and greeted their new commander. So much for Col Rowe's introduction to Bien Hoa's 3rd SOS.

There were a couple of other characters. One was Maj. Jerry Bourgeois, a Navigator. Fun to fly with whenever. So, one night he starts cussing us over the intercom, the pilots, for eating his M&M's that he had in his bag, and then leaving the wrapper. Of course, we denied any knowledge of the act. Well, he stewed, and later back in Ops he was looking at his nav bag. "What the heck?" "There is a hole in it." Now, we all knew there were critters that lived on the airplane. We figured one sniffed the candy, went into the bag, ate them, and then chewed its way out. See Jerry, it wasn't us.

There was one day in March when Jerry was very serious. A group was in the lounge, it was evening. The siren sounded, and we rushed for the rear door, which opened onto one of the four entrances of the sand bag revetment. Pushing and yelling, we got into the revetment. A few stragglers followed. Rockets crashed and exploded around our area, we figured big ones, 155mm. They made a particular noise as some passed overhead, some tumbling. Most of us got down on the floor. The sand bag walls were thick, but these were large rockets, not the smaller 107mm rockets. The shelling kept up for a few minutes.

We could see flickering in the open doorway facing away from our hooch. But no one wanted to go out to look figuring, one rocket burst might catch you in the door way. There was this continuing noise of something passing overhead. It sounded like rockets. Now Jerry, who had been in country longer than most of us, laid on the ground, up against a sandbag wall muttering "This is not good, not good". Most of us were seated on the floor. We continued to hear booms, and these "Woop-woop-woop" noises for several minutes.

The "All Clear" was finally given and we went back inside. Our hooch was relatively secure, as the first five feet of exterior wall was poured concrete. Here is the story. About a block away, there was a large warehouse building on fire. After the large building took a hit, supplies inside caught fire. However, the building also contained a large supply of bottled gasses, like oxygen, acetylene, and other pressurized gasses contributing to the intensity of the fire as they exploded. Many of the bottles did not explode, but rocketed out of the building with sufficient velocity to become airborne. It was those bottles we heard as they exited. The "Woop-woop" sound was the tumbling gas bottles.

As an officer there were benefits. In each of our rooms, we had a refrigerator with a freezer. We could keep soda's, beer, chocolates, cheese, whatever cold. One of the mysteries was the great steaks, one inch porterhouse steaks. Where they came from, I never asked. They would just appear.

A couple of industrious men, again scrounged some bricks and cement and built a cooking grill, along with a steel grill. Now to the charcoal. We traded. A case of coke was $2.40. We would give Jung two cases of coke, which she would strap to her scooter at the end of day. Off she would go. The next day she would appear and strapped to her scooter would be a large bag of Vietnamese charcoal. I used to think the bag was bigger than her. Scooter were great haulers of everything, from produce to families. I think we must have gotten some potatoes to bake from someplace. I never asked. Steaks were delicious.

I need to interject a story here. The Enlisted men did not enjoy the same luxuries. They were always having to "Make do." On one particular day, three of them decided to go to the Saigon docks to see what they could find. They had an Air Force pickup truck. While there they came upon a wooden case with "Frigidaire" stenciled on it. What blind luck! With some effort they tipped the case into the pickup and left the area like they knew what they were doing.

They arrived back at Bien Hoa, gloating over their bounty, and went right to their quarters. There they managed to pry open the case, nail by nail, and inside they found their booty. An aluminum gasoline engine. No refrigerator.

Now what to do? Forethought prevailed and the case was nailed back together. It was decided to take the prize over to Long Binh, and park the truck near the Marine area, as the Marines had a reputation for stealing anything. Carefully removing the vehicle keys to prevent its theft, they left the area for a period of time. Sure enough, when they returned, there was the truck, tailgate down, with the case gone. Tailgate secured, they drove off, mission accomplished.

It is now approaching the end of January. I have been in country four months.

I was no longer the designated Jeep driver. The "new guy" had the duty now, as I would climb in to the back seat. Front right would come later.

I have to relate a story now. Some new "Staff Weenie" decided he was going to get under control all of these errant Jeeps running around using the military gasoline. We had two liberated "US Army" jeeps. Jeeps like ours were the "grease" that kept everything running smoothly. Trips to the BX, haircut, chow hall, even operations were every day events, generally planned in advance. The gasoline access was through a white plastic "credit card" put into the pump. Suddenly all current cards were cancelled, and only approved vehicles could get new ones.

Much like "Mash" all hills can be overcome. A quick visit to our Spooky maintenance Sargent got us a couple lengths of rubber hose. Underwing, each Spooky fuel tank had a tank drain point that was used to check the fuel for water. Push up on it and fuel would come out into a catch container for a quick visual. The Spooky's all ran on AV gas, not jet fuel. So, and generally a two-man operation, pull the Jeep under the plane, remove the gas cap, and insert the hose. With the other end, push the valve up with the hose. You would get about a ¼" stream of gas. It would take a couple of minutes to get a good measure on the gas gauge. The Jeeps ran fine on AV gas.

The program lasted a couple of months. Soon the cards were so mixed up, stolen, whatever, that all control was lost, and we were back to our usual gas fill up's. One thing I liked about combat and the American service men, somebody always has a deal. Sort of like our steaks, or fresh bread.

TRAN VAN ANH

I want to include a personal story. One of our in-flight translators was Anh, **Tran Van Anh**, a very personable gentleman. He and I developed a friendship. He was a few years older than me, educated, and has been a high school history teacher. Because he was educated, he was an officer, one of the few who flew with us. I think all the aircrewmen liked him because he would pitch in and help reload, whatever.

"An", as he became known to me spent hours telling me how Viet Nam used to be before the war. He also related back to the French era, and the education system. The French controls were very subjective and demeaning. For examples, school students were forbidden to speak

Vietnamese, but had to converse and write in French. Classrooms were very rigid, and the students wore uniforms.

Anh loaned me books to read, in French, which at the time, I could read and translate. He gave me a great knowledge about Vietnam.

One thing, you can name the city "Ho Chi Minh" City, but it will always be Saigon. No pollical entity has ever been able to control the agrarian South Vietnam. Vietnam has been invaded and fought over by numerous forces, be they Chinese, Japanese, and later the French. And soon the North Vietnamese forces, who will not be welcomed there. The South will prevail.

I wonder what was the post war fate if Anh, and of course my Ve and Jung?

CHAPTER 7
SPOOKY OPERATIONS

From my September arrival through December 1968, time passed quickly. I was learning how to be a contributing crewmember. Col. Hyde was a regimented pilot and went seriously about his inflight duties. He expected his copilot to know his duties also. He never said much, just nodded when what he expected to be done was done. Gear up, gear down, flaps, tailwheel, and fuel management were to just be completed. I was airborne about 100 hours a month, with "Wheel time", actually flying the airplane, perhaps 45 hours a month, in CAP duties.

With the rainy season, there was little action. I would get bored just flying so I made up some exercises to do. I would practice instrument flying by turning right 10 degrees, at ten degrees of bank, and when I reached the ten degrees off course, I would reverse direction, sweeping over centerline to ten degrees in the opposite direction. I decided to add complexity. Maintaining a constant power setting, I would climb one hundred feet, and then lighten the wheel pressure, allowing the plane to descend to 100 feet below course. Then start back up again. So, then I would do them both together, turning and climbing and descending. I don't think anyone ever noticed. And Hyde said nothing. At the end of the course, and to maintain the CAP configuration, I would enter into a standard rate turn and reverse course. There were no other aircraft in our area.

In December, the Squadron had an incident, that could have resulted in the loss of an aircraft. The Spooky was undertaking a flare dropping mission. An OV-10 FAC (Forward Air Controller), was diving and marking targets for most likely F-100's on a bombing run. Flying into the flare light, which was described as a "Milk Bowl" of light caused night vision to be lost. The Spooky was running a standard left turn drop pattern. As the Fac was climbing out after a marking run, in travel opposite to Spooky, he ran into the Spooky fuselage at the wing root and landing gear area, and rolled around the Spooky with its propeller cutting into the fuselage in front of the tail, and then flew off into the night. There were no crewmembers on the Spooky injured, but the OV-10 pilots lost their lives. The Spooky managed to fly back to Bien Hoa, where they skidded off of the foamed runway, gear up. The crew was able to exit the aircraft with limited injuries. I believe Major Reeder was the aircraft commander and Lt. Pete Rose was copilot. Pete and I later served together at a follow-on assignment at Wurtsmith AFB, Michigan.

There were other close calls. I will relate mine. In March, I believe, as Spooky 71, we were supporting a bombing mission with flares. There were several F-100 aircraft, all anxious to drop their loads. After this one particular bomb run, the F-100 pulled up through the flare "Milk-Bowl" effect, rotating left, exposing its bottom in the climb. The F-100 came so close in passing by our aircraft nose, I could count the rivets. Pure good fortune. The Hun Driver never knew.

There was another sad incident in what I believe was January 1969. Sad because it really hurt the spirit of a fine officer and Spooky pilot. The aircraft commander was a career Major. He was providing flare support for a group of APCs (Armored Personnel Carriers) were under attack by the VC. The Spooky was dropping flares, as requested, which kept the VC at bay. It was requested that Spooky clear a travel path forward, by shooting about 100 yards and further out. The 100 yards is close work, but feasible. As a reminder, the Spooky was flying at 3000 feet above the ground at night, under flare light. Now men in the lead APC vehicle decided they wanted to see the Spooky fire, and got out of their APC and were up on it to watch. The Spooky began accurately firing, and ricochet bullets flew in the direction of the men, wounding some. Upon notification the Spooky ceased firing, and withdrew. The Spooky returned to base and landed. A "Short Round", aka "Friendly-Fire" incident report was filed. After incident investigation, the Spooky pilot was cleared of any wrongdoing, and returned to duty.

The Holidays were behind us, now early January. We were wresting with the flare issue. I don't remember who was the aircraft commander was, however, soon after takeoff, we were diverted to fly to an Artillery Firebase under attack in the North of III Corps. The firebase was located not far from the Cambodian border. It came under mortar attack on a regular basis. I noted that many attacks occurred on a Saturday night, and separated by a two-week period. I used to joke that it was a downrange point for a mortar school.

Many North Vietnamese troops were moving south. They came down through Laos and then Cambodia. Rainy season was over, so they and equipment could move. Their apparent objective was to overrun this isolated firebase. The Vietnamese began their assault at dusk with ground troops assaulting the wire surroundings of the base. I think now they were high on drugs because their objective was to sacrifice themselves, falling on the barbed wire as they died, making a channel for those behind them to funnel through, stepping on their bodies. The follow through troops were sappers, carrying satchel charges to throw into the compound bunkers. Often, they would blow themselves up.

We arrived and immediately dropping flares. Firebases are obvious, a sterile brown circular area, devoid of vegetation, usually located on high ground. The Army ground radio communications was extremely heavy, excited, with a lot of shouting. We broke in, and they were excited to have our support, noting the light from flares. "Spooky, shoot anywhere, they are coming through the wire..." We confirmed they were all in bunkers and fighting positions. They were advised that we were going to start firing inside the grounds, "Do it, do it" was the response, obviously under stress.

This time two guns were brought on line, slow fire rate. I flipped the cover on the overhead firing switch, "Switch on". Firing began, working near the center. The tracer stream was heavy. There was no ground fire directed at us that I could see. The guns are controlled from the back. To get two, or more, guns online, that has to be requested over the intercom. Two had been requested. After firing a couple of bursts with two guns, the aircraft commander said "Let's go with one gun", and one gun was switched off. We continued firing, working around in a circular pattern. Apparently, the troops on the ground could hear our bullets hitting their bunkers, because from time to time they offered their "Keep it up, Spooky" over the radio. After a few minutes, and a lot of double flares, we reported that we had swept the inside area. We now were ready to start working outside the wire, hoping to catch the now retreating attack VC's.

We were advised they had an OP (Observation Post) outside the wire and wanted to bring the two-man team in. Such posts are designed to watch for enemy movement, and report. Usually, the OP's are vacated before an attack. This time the attacking NVA moved past them to attack. They just stayed under cover.

We agreed to hold fire, continuing to drop flares for illumination. After a long minute, we were told they were inside the wire and men were moving outside their bunkers. We were cleared to fire anyplace outside the wire., which we did. The Firebase advised there was a stream, and more than likely a retreat route. The Nav reported that it didn't show up on his map. We fired around the base for a few minutes, and then gave the men in back a chance to catch up, and focused on flare drops.

We did not expect a further attack that night, and that we would soon be out of flares. We advised the Firebase and they concurred. They said they would take over using artillery illum rounds. And they thanked us. We headed back to base for reassignment, as necessary.

He following day we were advised of a BDA count, a body count, a sizeable number. The VC outside the wire, probably carried off their dead and wounded.

Such reports bothered me. I was not interested in score keeping, leave that to others. What satisfied me was that were had done our jobs, and broken up the attack. One Firebase saved for another day, and night.

That closed out January. I was into my fifth month. There were a lot of crew changes. Because of the one-year rotation, 8% of the crewmembers rotated home each month. And there were R&R's, (Rest and Relaxation) which took a crewmember out for a week. I realized my R&R would be coming up in a month or so.

February 1969 started quietly for us. Intel reported troop movement of men and material down the trail. I can't remember any specific events, mostly flare missions. The bad lot of flares was behind us, as we could now drop one at a time. We could provide illumination all evening, unless called off to elsewhere. Troops on the ground appreciated having us there.

In writing this, I realized that I rarely was on a crew for the Spooky 73 sorties, the midnight launch. Usually, I went up as Spooky 71, which was the 7PM launch. I was on a Spooky 72 once, the backup for Spooky 71. Could it be because I was teamed with senior officers? No telling.

Just for orientation, the 3rd Special Operations Squadron, Bien Hoa, was to plan four missions, "Sorties", every day. They were to be Spooky 71 through Spooky 74. Each of the operational bases throughout Vietnam and Thailand has specific numbers assigned to them. For Bien Hoa, Spooky 71 was the first sortie, and Spooky 72 was its back up. Then Spooky 73 was the midnight sortie, with Spooky 74 its backup. Once assigned the plane and crew would carry the number assignment throughout the night. For example, if Spooky 71 was assigned to a target, expended its flares, came back and reloaded, it would take off again as Spooky 71.

There was also a 4th Special Operations Squadron, based in the Northern half of Vietnam. For example, Spooky's flying out of the Northernmost base, Danang, was Spooky 10 through 14.

Vietnam was full of characters. I know as I flew a Spooky 73 series, taking off at midnight flying until dawn, Dawn was breaking in Vietnam and there was a radio call over the Emergency Radio Frequency, UHF 243.0, which is usually reserved for true emergencies. All military aircraft monitor this frequency. Loud and clear came through "Buck, Buck, It's Chickenman! Good Morning, Vietnam!" Chickenman was a personal callsign of a FAC (Forward Air Controller) who patrolled at dawn for any targets in his area. The aircraft would have been a military O1A, single engine Piper or Cessna. He would be armed with a few smoke rockets and perhaps smoke grenades, in the event he found a lucrative target, and fighter bombers could be called on to strike it.

So much for early morning hours. A little combat humor.

Then there are quaint names for areas on maps that had particular shapes, usually where significant firefights took place. A couple of names, "Angel's Wing", "Parrots Beak" and "Dogs Head". To a veteran, they bring back memories.

CHAPTER 8
PRELUDE

February moved quickly. Hooch life was good. I did a lot of bridge playing on days off, steaks, and O'Club meals. Sundays were schedule make-up day, and always liked looking over the shoulder of the Scheduling Officer, sometimes teasing. I'd see four on, three off, and the AC's name. The Nav was also assigned. Our team.

This particular Monday, 24 February, there was a new name, a new Aircraft Commander "Carpenter". I did not know him, never met, nor had I seen him around the "day" room. No big deal, it was just another CAP mission. I think Charlie Haigh and Pete Rose were assigned to Spooky 73.

Typical day, left for Operations at five, six PM briefing, quiet night forecast. Same troop movements. The weather was clear, no moon, just a routine mission. I can't remember Major Ken Carpenter at the briefing, perhaps he sat behind me. Picked up my gear, in-flight meal and rode out to the plane. Tail number assigned, 770, we pulled up and off loaded. Spooky 72 went to their plane to preflight, as did 73 and 74. Get it done while still light.

The back-end crew was waiting by the cargo door. They were SSgt. Edward Fuzie, Sgt. Thomas Baer, A1C Ellis C. Owen and A1C John L.

Levitow. Levitow had swapped sorties with another Loadmaster. No big deal. The Nav, Major William Platt, and I walked up and said hello. I don't know where he came from, as Major Kenneth Carpenter joined us, and we greeted him. First impression, he was perhaps 5'8", dark hair. He seemed a little nervous, as he asked a couple of questions. He saw were there and asked "Where is our VC", which struck me. Our Vietnamese Observer replied "Here I am", standing there from the beginning.

I had come to respect our Vietnamese Observers. First, I had gotten to know Sgt. Anh, and second, they put their lives on the line waiting to be of service, and usually had to sit on the canvas seat by the bulkhead on flights. They were trained to work as a liaison between the American aircrew and Vietnamese combat units. Most pitched in when asked, otherwise they kept out of the way. I think Carpenters nervousness made him make the comment.

I came to learn later that this was his very first mission without an experienced IP. I may have been assigned because of my experience. It was obvious he knew his way around the aircraft operation, but wish he would have told us at the pre-flight. So, with an "OK, let's go", we boarded the plane. Carpenter did the walk around and I set up the cockpit, so when he came forward, I was settling in my seat. He belted in to his seat, and asked "Ready". It was obvious that Major Carpenter was comfortable with the aircraft operation and we were soon ready to take off.

Major Carpenter was a career officer. He entered the officer ranks through the Air Force Cadet Program and had previously been an enlisted airman. Once an Air Cadet, he was able to go to pilot training, and had several thousand hours in propeller cargo aircraft, including C-47's.

Spooky 71 took off on time and flew to, and entered, the Saigon Cap. Mixtures were set at auto-lean, and we were running out of the aft tanks. I then took over and flew the first hour, we then rotated hourly, ending up about 11:45PM, ready to return to Bien Hoa. The evening had been totally quiet. We heard the call from Spooky 73 to control that they were enroute to take over the Cap. We made a departure call.

Hillsboro Control responded with an assignment to proceed to Long Binh for a report of a probe in the barbed wire at the edge of the base. We were given a contact name and frequency. We arrived a few minutes after midnight on Tuesday, February 25th, and made contact. The back-end crew had been alerted and had flares ready. The Gunners, Baer and Owen, had the miniguns loaded, in the event they were called on.

Carpenter circled the site and called for a flare. Levitow had set the timer on the first flare. We were at 3000 feet of altitude above the ground and he set the timers at "Five and Five" our standard. This meant that five seconds after release and the firing pin pulled, a fifteen-foot parachute would pop out of the tube. In another five seconds the magnesium flare would ignite. The flare would be about 2500 feet above the ground and provide light for two minutes, long enough for us to loop our racetrack pattern and release another flare. The flare itself was so bright that you could not directly look into it. On this evening, Ellis Owen, was in the open cargo door, on his knees, hooking the cargo strap to the safety lanyard, pulling the cross-safety pin and pitching the flare down and to the rear into the slipstream.

The cargo strap was anchored to an anchor ring on the floor. It allowed the flare strap to go to full length beyond the aircraft elevator, before the lanyard and firing pin was pulled. The Airman would then pull the strap in, and make ready for the next flare release. Visually, they could not track the target location, so had to be ready to hook and pitch another flare on command to "Drop Flare".

This two-man operation was well rehearsed by each of the men, and handling the 36-inch Mark 24, five-inch diameter flare tube weighing 27 pounds, no easy task. It took both hands to control it, momentarily releasing one hand to hook the cargo strap.

Copilot Slocum looked over Carpenters shoulder and looked out the pilot's side window at the illuminated area. All was quiet, and there was no report of activity. Carpenter asked for and received a release to fire the miniguns in the target area.

As a matter of practice, Slocum quickly checked the fuel in each tank, and continued running on the rear aux tanks.

Carpenter confirmed the target with the navigator, who was looking out his side window in the target area. Carpenter planned on using one gun, and copilot Slocum flipped the overhead safety switch on and advised ready to fire. As a matter of practice, he kept his hand on the safety cover, ready to snap it closed, if warranted.

Carpenter fired about a five second burst and adjusted his firing circle. Aware of his flare time, called for another flare. The Spooky then fired another burst, a little longer this time. There were two more short bursts into the target area. There was no return fire or ground fire noted. Slocum snapped the fire switch off.

There was perhaps thirty second of active firing time, 1500 rounds and five or six flares released.

The radio call came, "Spooky 71", and answered by the navigator, Maj. Platt. It was now perhaps fifteen minutes after midnight on the 25th. "We have a troop in contact for you" and giving him co-ordinates and a contact name. Troops in contact was a priority mission, an active shooting fire fight between opposing forces. The Nav consulted his map and told us it was northeast of Saigon, perhaps twenty minutes away.

Carpenter and Slocum reviewed the fuel situation. There was thirty gallons in each of the main tanks, and a little less in the rear aux tanks. Less than 100 gallons, significant only that Spooky 71 took off with about 800 gallons on board.

Slocum elected to run on the rear aux tanks and monitor the fuel levels. Carpenter concurred, and set his props to 1600 rpm, an endurance RPM, for fuel conservation. They headed to the target and advised the back-end crew they were headed to a "Troops in Contact" Target. That meant load and make ready all three guns.

At this point enroute that Carpenter asked navigator Platt if he had requested artillery clearance. Platt responded positively "On request". It was then that Spooky 71 was advised that they would be supporting a South Vietnamese firebase. This meant the Vietnamese observer would be utilized, and he was summoned forward, as communication would be in Vietnamese.

Co-pilot Slocum, looking over his left shoulder, observed him, reviewing the navigators map. He had his headset on. By then they were approaching the target area. About ten miles out, it was obvious that it was an active firefight, with multicolored tracers firing in both directions observed in the clear night sky, along with white explosive flashes. Green tracers, 51 caliber Chinese made, were fired by the VC and ricocheted into the air, most likely off of armored vehicles. In return, the South Vietnamese fired the American made 50 caliber orange tracer rounds. The firefight was intense.

The Vietnamese observer had moved forward, and was standing in the cockpit doorway, ducking down, intently looking out the front windshield. At five miles, Copilot Slocum commented to Carpenter about the intensity of the fight and the explosive flashes, as Carpenter flew the airplane to favor the South Vietnamese area of the target, making left hand turns easier. The Observer said nothing about the target. We had not made radio contact with them.

The scene was now set. It was about 12:30AM, on Tuesday, February 25th.

CHAPTER 9
FLASH!! BANG!!

It was like a giant hand that reached out and stopped the airplane in flight. A shock had gone through the plane on impact, but not violent. My first reaction was "I've run this out of gas!", but a quick look down by my left knee at the gas gauge showed 20 gallons with gauge knob in the correct position. I thought this because as an engine ran lean before stopping, it would backfire through the intake scoop. But the flash I perceived out of the corner of my eye was a large one.

The cockpit began to darken to a yellow glow. Glancing at the engine RPM's showed that they had slowed to 1200 RPM, both engines, and since the C-47 had generators, the voltage had fallen off. The nose of the plane was beginning to rise, as if the airplane was squatting. My right hand was on the yoke, fingers split, one above the spoke, the others below. along with the push to transmit button unit. A single black wire, about ¼ inch in diameter, ran four feet long to the transmit button, and a second section about two feet in length ran from transmit button to my headset connection plug.

The plane sounded labored with the RPM's at 1200, nose rising. I turned and looked over at Major Carpenter, and his chin was on his upper chest, head down, eyes partially open, and his right arm draped to his side, the left off the control wheel. He was either dead or knocked out cold. I took the wheel with both hands momentarily, and then with my right hand reached up overhead and flipped the radio switch, to the Guard frequency, 243.0, and the IFF to Emergency, still holding the transmit button block.

I had some feel for the plane as the right wing was beginning to drop off to the right. Airspeed was at 60 knots in the dimmed light, nose still rising. The sky was clear, no moon, and very few stars visible. Pushing the transmit button, I called out "Mayday! Mayday! This is Spooky 71 and we have taken a hit from a big gun, and are going down. Maybe a 37 millimeter at our present position. Eight souls on board". There was an acknowledgement of the call out that I cannot remember, as I was now focused on our 45 degree nose up attitude, with a right wing droop. I was letting the plane take its own course as the nose rose. Again, the maneuver was not violent, but rather almost in slow motion.

Reaching out with my left hand, I moved the mixture knobs from auto lean to rich, and then reached over to the prop handles and pushed them forward. There was a little grumble and a "wah-wha" as the prop pitch changed, and the engine rpms synchronized. I left the throttles in place, more from not knowing what to do, throttle up or throttle back. Now the aircraft was about 75 degrees nose up, falling off to the right and slowly turning right. There were no visual references, with the exception of a very few ground lights I saw in my peripheral vision.

I don't know why it came to mind at the time, a there is pilot training maneuver called a "Lazy Eight" in which the pilot lowers the nose to gain some airspeed, then pull back on the stick or yoke, pulling the nose through the horizon while simultaneously starting a roll to the left or right. The well-executed maneuver, would have the aircraft at the zenith of the curve, having turned 90 degrees from its original direction, wings vertical, fuselage parallel to the ground. The airspeed should be almost at stall speed knots. Then the pilot would allow the nose to lower, still continuing the change in direction, airspeed to increase and begin a slow roll out. This is all done as one continuous, always changing, maneuver, so that the airplane had turned 180 degrees from the original heading, ending at the starting altitude and airspeed. The maneuver could also be demonstrated, continuing on, but in the opposite direction. To the casual reader, it is very similar to a roller coaster ride. A well-executed lazy eight would load the aircraft very slightly, perhaps 1.2 or 1.3 "G" s.

Spooky 71 was now gaining speed. The nose was down perhaps 30 degrees. I think that I saw 140 knots. The most significant thing was the "Howl" that started, the sound that WWII bombers made as they fell from the sky, as the props over sped. I had the left rudder depressed, feeding in aileron with a wheel turn. Early on, and at a lower speed, the wheel was approaching 90 degrees of turn, now down around 45 degrees. The wings, and thus the plane was now, nose down, level with the horizon. In my head I thought "I can still fly this thing". I continued to draw back on the wheel, ever mindful that I did not know the condition of the wing, and certainly didn't want to fold the wing up. Because I had aileron control, I knew the cables were intact. There are no hydraulic controls on a C47, all are operated by cables.

I continued to gently load the plane. Because the plane and thus the wings, were now level to the horizon, albeit 30 degrees nose down, the lift vector was now vertical, meaning that all the lift was to raise the nose. We went through 150 knots as the nose approached level flight. Finally Spooky 71 levelled. I had rudder force in, and continued to reach down and rotate the rudder trim knob, trying to relieve my foot and leg pressure. Some aileron pressure was needed to keep the right wing up. I saw 160 knots and 2200 feet of altitude, level fight.

As I said in the beginning of this chapter, much seemed to take place in slow motion. Spooky 71 had turned 180 degrees, reversing course. My estimate of time now, was at least a minute and a half from start to finish, wings level. The time to read this chapter.

Major Carpenter had not moved. He was still out. For the first time, I turned left and looked down the length of the airplane. Gone was our in-flight Viet observer, who was in the cockpit doorway, and what I saw was our back-end crew lying in a pile over each other, to the right of the ammo cans. . Significantly to me was the layers of smoke, three layers, filling the fuselage.

Traveling forward with my eyes, on the left hand side, I knew there were first aid kits and parachutes hung on the wall, even though I could not see them. Chest parachutes. The thought of bailing out passed through my mind, but I realized that I had to keep flying the plane, holding the controls in place. There was no bailing out.

A call came over the radio, "Spooky 71, Spooky 73". It was our airborne replacement that had taken off at midnight, to take our place in the cap. I recognized the voice of Captain Charlie Haigh, and also Lt. Pete Rose, co-pilot. They asked what happened and I briefed them. "All are down in the back, and Major Carpenter is unconscious. I'm flying the plane." There may have been more chit-chat, unremembered by me. They were on the way to our target which was a hot site. I'm sure I advised it was a Viet firefight and plan to use their interpreter.

Then a call came from Dust-off, Army emergency medical helicopters. "Spooky, understand you have wounded on board", and I confirmed we did. "We'll follow you back". Great. I told them that I did not know the condition of the landing gear and tire, and would not be surprised if the airplane "Ground Looped" on touchdown, spinning off the runway to the right. Followed by, "And if there was a fire, blow the flames forward, as the exit would be through the removed cargo door on the port side rear".

About then Major Carpenter began to regain consciousness. I told him we had been hit by an a "Arty" round. His whit's coming back to him, he looked over and sat up in the seat saying. "I'll take the airplane". I quickly briefed him on the condition of the plane, running on the rear fuel tanks with an estimated 15 gallons of gas in each. I told him I was still holding in heavy left rudder, and relinquished the controls as I felt my rudder pedal load diminish. His first comment was "That's Ben Hoa right off the nose". Really it was ten miles away. I looked out to my left for the first time and could see the Saigon River and a few city lights. It was well after midnight. We were still at 2200 feet.

By Carpenter taking over, I was able to check check things out. All looked good. I flipped the fuel tank indicator to the left aux, it showed about 15 gallons, matching the right tank. Flipped again, left front main, 30 gallons, and right main, the same. The C47 had self-sealing tanks, so either they were sealed or had not suffered any shrapnel hits. In my mind, I decided to run the aux tanks to final approach, then switch to the mains for landing.

Carpenter tried to turn to look back, but could not. Over the intercom, he inquired their status. I believe it was Sgt. Levitow who responded, that Sgt. Baer and Sgt. Fuzie were badly wounded. Levitow then said "The flares were beginning to smoke". Carpenter's immediate response was "Ditch them!" He then got up and picked each one out of the box and threw them out of the open cargo door. Perhaps 28 to 30 flares, smoking or not.

Even though he was wearing his light weight, leather palmed, flight gloves, his hands were scorched from the heat being generated by the smoking flares.

About four minutes had now passed from the initial hit. I decided to get off Guard frequency. At the same time, Major Carpenter inquired of the navigator's status over the intercom. The Navigators position was on the port side, behind Major Carpenters position. There was front emergency exit door directly behind Carpenter, then the Nav's station. The navigator, Major Platt responded that he was OK. Major Carpenter then told him to get a couple of First Aid kits and go back to the rear and help. "And get the Viet too."

The first aid kits were hung on the port side wall behind the parachutes. Several of them on the wall labelled "First Aid".

The UHF radios are well designed. Along the top front there are four thumb knobs. Knob up, vertical, is the zero position, and then by rotating the knob with your fingers, each clocked around to the nine position. Thus, a pilot could set in a known frequency without looking. All our UHF frequencies began with a two or three, and ended with a decimal and a tenth value.

In the radio center was a large paddle knob with stations. Again clocked. Station one was a common ground frequency. Two, tower, three departure, and four o'clock tactical. Five might be airborne control. My overhead radio was on four, tactical. I expected the Dustoff's would be also. "Dustoff, Spooky 71 going to Approach."

Now the Army troops on the ground, who we had not spoken with, had FM radios at a lower frequency, so no concern with them. They could not hear the conversations.

"Bien Hoa Approach, Spooky 71 Emergency". I heard the Dustoff say "Dustoff 10", so I knew they were keeping up and tracking us. Bien Hoa Approach replied they were tracking our radar beacon. I responded that we had four wounded crewmembers on board. Little more was said.

The Nav was in the back attending to the wounded men. There was no conversation with them. Major Carpenter had pulled the prop's levers back to where he wanted them and adjusted the throttles. I advised the current fuel situation and my plans to use the fuel. It had been perhaps ten minutes since the hit, but seemed longer. Bien Hoa as at the ten o'clock position as we reduced altitude to about a thousand feet, about 800 feet above ground level, and began a sweeping left turn. Airspeed about 130 knots.

CHAPTER 10
APPROACH AND LANDING

Spooky 71 was under Bien Hoa Approach Radar, flying tactical, I had turned off the IFF Emergency Squawk on the transponder. Save it for the next emergency. It was a very clear night. We were flying at a thousand feet, about 800 feet AGL, 130 knots. Saigon was off my left shoulder.

After over two minutes, Major Carpenter was now appearing alert and ready to start flying again. He took control. We began to discuss the "What if's", wondering about the condition of the wheels, especially the right tire. What about a ground loop on touchdown? As a relatively low time co-pilot, I had never experienced one, nor seen one. Was it a slow or fast event? A ground loop was not a totally uncommon experience, even among experienced pilots, and would have been mostly an embarrassment for the pilot, as there was little damage, if any. But with wounded on board, a different story, as they were not belted down.

We were still flying on the aux fuel tanks. I checked and told Carpenter my plan to switch over to the main tanks, still holding 30 gallons each. If we had to go around, I wanted plenty of fuel. The AC 47 has self-sealing bladder tanks, so even if hit, were supposed to retain fuel. Ours appeared fine.

Engine-tank feed is controlled by valve knobs on the left and right side of the console. On the right, at about belt high, was the Right Main Tank and the Rear Auxiliary Tank positions. On the left side, next to the Aircraft Commander, was the left side identical selections. All I had to do was reach over and make the selection. There are other fuel options, that I am not getting into here. The AC47 had fuel boost pumps, so I turn them on. The switches were over my head, and normally off in flight, except when changing fuel tank feed. I turned the fuel gauge selector knob to Left Main, and switched the valve to Left Main. I liked to wait ten to twenty seconds to make sure the engine fuel feed was uninterrupted. I turned the gauge knob to the Right Main, and did the same. Then I rotated the gauge knob around to Left Main, and turned off the boost pumps. Task complete.

It was time to lower the landing gear. Floor levers were moved to open valves and allow the gear to drop. Two thumps indicated down and the hydraulic pressure moved back to 800 PSI, down and locked. The cockpit indicators showed the same. But still the tire....

We were now about five miles out, lined up for the approach, assigned to the runway, a single runway. Light winds, smooth air. Carpenter now asked for wing flaps. Again, to the floor, and I began to "Milk" them down, not knowing if the right flap and/or mechanism had been damaged. If damaged it could cause the airplane to yaw or roll. Half flaps, so far, all good. Observing this, I continued to feed them down to full flaps.

Carpenter then began to reduce power to reach a glide path approach. He was looking for about 100 knots, planning to fly the approach at 80 knots. But the airplane began to shudder, and we could feel it. Perhaps because of the flaps down and airspeed reduction, the wing angle of attack exposed the hole in the wing to air flow, disrupting it. Carpenter asked "Do you feel that?" Of course, I did.

Carpenter, advanced the throttles a little, moving back to 120 knots, shudder gone. But we were by now on glide path nose down slightly. He had to adjust his aim point towards the front of the overrun, or we would land long, down the runway. I Re-checked the "Before Landing" checklist, "Complete". Fuel boost pump switches to "On".

The crash vehicles were lined up, lights flashing, left side, near the beginning of the runway on the run-up area. Five hundred feet, four hundred, walking the throttles back, three hundred, then two, on centerline, about a hundred feet, rotating to almost level flight, we entered the "Ground Effect" air at about fifty feet, still over the chevron striped overrun at the beginning of the runway. Ground effect is an atmospheric compression of landing air by the wings, and aids in a smooth landing.

Carpenter and I were both thinking to same thought, and were tensed, waiting for touchdown. The picture out the windshield looked good. The final glide was smooth.

"Bump, bump" the tires touched down and we rolled straight ahead. **Intact!!** Carpenter slid his feet up the pedals and evenly applied the toe brakes, slowing. By now we both had let out our held breath, and were feeling much more at ease. He allowed the tail wheel to lower and make contact. He then indicated he planned to turn off the runway at the first left taxiway, so I reached down and lifted the tail wheel lock lever, releasing the tail wheel swivel. We turned left and rolled onto the connecting taxiway. I released the lever, and sat up. We were between the runway and main taxiway. Emergency vehicles were approaching from behind us.

We came to a stop midway on the connecting taxiway. I think we both felt pretty good about our efforts and procedures. I was gathering up my papers and checklist, flashlight, and did a quick check. Suddenly a fully-garbed rescue fireman filled the doorway between us and said "All the wounded are off the plane, and onto the Dustoff's…" "You all can get off." We thanked him and he turned around and left.

It was then that one of the memorable landing events occurred. Carpenter and I looked at each other and smelled the strong odor of alcohol. "It must be from the anti-icing system". The fluid was never removed before the plane was sent to the tropical combat zone. The explosion had ruptured the system allowing it to leak, and when parked, it ran in such a way to enter the fuselage, the vapors rising to our noses.

Major Carpenter got up from his seat and headed out, with me following. Looking around there was not much to see until we reached the 7.62mm ammunition containers, still strapped to the floor. Working around them, I saw the empty flare box, and noted the blood on the floor, making it very slippery. The cargo door opening was clear, and the small exit ladder in place. Down it and I was on the ground.

I walked around the tail of the plane, looking it over. There was not much light, no spotlights, just light from the vehicles. Looking at the fuselage, I could not see much. Mostly small holes in the dark exterior.

Looking now at the right wing, and there it was, perhaps a 20-inch hole, some metal rolled back and a black soot teardrop pattern towards the rear of the wing. The hole was perhaps thirty inches from the right engine nacelle and twenty-four inches from the trailing edge. A second later in flight and it would have missed us. The what ifs: Thirty inches to the left, and a foot forward, and it would have taken out the right engine. Five feet left and it would have taken out the front-end crew. I am thankful.

CHAPTER 11
THE DAYS AFTER AND
HONG KONG

Tuesday, 25 February -- I stopped by the Squadron Operations about 2AM. Lights on, but there was nobody in Operations.

As of January 1969, and the result of "Short Round" concerns, all the Spooky aircraft were fitted, at the Nav's station, with a simple Sony tape recorder. When we received a call from Command, the Nav was to press the "Record" paddles. Thus, all instructions would be recorded. And again, when a Spooky received target information as well as all the time on target.

Operations had spare recorders and wires. I wish I had made a duplicate copy of our mission by playing the original tape into a second recorder. Alas, I did not. And the original tape? Gone for the ages.

Soon a crew came in. It was Spooky 74, and they were in crew rest in the trailer. Our target was still a hot target, and they were to take off and relieve Spooky 73, who was running low on flares. I seriously considered, logging on with them to go up again. Sort of "Get back on the horse that threw you". But they slipped out and I was getting tired. I got a ride back to the hooch for some sleep.

I got up late that morning, and checked the schedule. There was a new crew assigned to Spooky 71, and I was not on the board. I showered and dressed in the garb of the day, a flight suit. It was everyday dress for flight crews, so nothing special. I hitched a ride out to the flight line, but nothing there. I learned the plane was still parked on the taxiway from the night before. I asked for a ride to the taxiway location, and found it was easier to take a squadron jeep.

Arriving at the plane there was a few men looking at the plane. They were all enlisted men, maintenance men it appeared to me. So, there it was, the right wing with about a 20-inch hole, and black soot mark trailing rearward. It was precariously close to the right aileron. Looking at the side of the airplane, there were windows blown out, but did not look to be in bad condition. I took a few pictures, and walked around the plane to the cargo door. The steps were in place, so I climbed in. There was blood on the floor, and somewhat slippery. Ammo cans were still tied down along the centerline. The flare box was open, but no flares.

Looking at the right interior fuselage, it looked like a sieve with all of the shrapnel holes with the sunlight to back it up. Amazing, with over 3500 shrapnel holes later reported. I picked up a small shrapnel piece off of the floor, a sector of a sealing ring that went around a mortar round, to seal the firing gasses required to eject the mortar round from the mortar tube.

Satisfied, I caught a ride back to Operations. Major Larry Janssen, the Operations Officer, was seated at his desk, and upon entering he said

"Lieutenant, Good Job, you had quite a night last night". And that was the only comment made to me. He followed up with, "Take a couple days off, and we'd like to give you a trip to Hong Kong". That surprised me a little, but nothing more was ever said.

To this day, I question in my mind why I was given a trip to Hong Kong.

In two days, I had TDY flight orders for Hong Kong, along with Major Janssen, as Aircraft Commander, a navigator and a flight engineer. A hotel assignment, meals, all courtesy of the Air Force.

Nha Trang was Spooky Headquarters and a major maintenance location. Aircraft were regularly ferried to Nha Trang and swapped for a post militance aircraft. Nha Trang was about an hour and a half flight north of Bien Hoa. So, we took one of our fleet to there to drop off. The following day, we picked up a plain gray military C-47 transport for our trip. The trip was published at base operations on the "Space Available" board, so we carried about six military members who wanted to go to Hong Kong.

Hong Kong was a pleasant opportunity to purchase a Nikon Camera and a Seiko watch. Plus, I had a shopping list of the wants of Squadron mates. The return flights were uneventful.

For me, the time was now April of 1969. I personally had other military adventures, yes, and I was shot at, yes, but they missed.

My brother was not drafted.

CHAPTER 12
BIEN HOA DAYS 1969

I was becoming seasoned. Get up each day and go do it. But there were breaks. I went with whatever crew needed a fill in. I just looked at the schedule board. I was becoming a veteran.

Hey, I could put in for R&R, now where did I sign up? I don't remember. I had decided that I wanted to go to Australia. A few of the married guys went to Hawaii, eh, I'll do that later. Bangkok, no, Hong Kong no.

I put in for a week and got it. Sydney, Australia, flight pre-paid. All I had to do was get to Saigon. I needed orders and a military ID. None of us had Passports. I can't remember how, but I got my flight. Maybe World Airways. I few to Perth, on the western end of Australia. There we all waited five or six hours for a change of planes. Departures were scheduled so as to arrive in Sydney at 8AM in the morning. I don't know how; I just got some Australian currency. I had my credit card for any big deals.

I don't think most Americans realize how big Australia actually is. West to East, same as USA. We boarded finally and flew all night. Finally, Sydney. Immigration was orderly. Stand in line, then step forward, hand the agent your orders and military ID. A quick look in your eyes, the agent then punches in a set of numbers, and then suit case show and tell.

After a quick check for Playboy Magazines, and contraband, off I went.

I was booked at the Wentworth Hotel, a Class A hotel. I think my six-day stay was about $360 Australian, perhaps $450 USA dollars. I went up, showered and went out to look around. It is said that Sydney is the mirror of San Francisco, and you know, it is. Except they drive and walk on the opposite side of the road and sidewalk. One has to watch stepping off of the curb. Look the other way.

I had decided to buy some wool goods. I found a men's store nearby. I will say this, the Australians are the nicest people in the world. Every store salesperson, manager, lit up as soon as I spoke. And you know what, they wanted to take you home for dinner, Yep, they did. Now my thoughts were "Got any daughters?' but I kept them to myself.

The hotel meals were fine. I was trying to find things to do. The front desk had a rack of entertainment. So first off, I signed up for a Grey Line City Tour to orient myself and learn about the city. Very Informative.

Sydney is a harbor city, and had tourist boat rides. I decided a five PM departure would be best. So, the end of my first day, a harbor tour.

There were others who had the same idea. Girls. They knew that the GI's were on R&R and they knew the plane schedules. Where to meet?

Bars and cruises. One girl caught my eye with her smile. Her two friends went of and we just talked. Susan, I believe. I told her I was terrible at names, but good at numbers. I told her that I had selected a nonsense number "Seven", and so she became Seven. She really didn't like it, but accepted it.

We talked all evening. She worked in a shop, and as I learned, regularly, cruised. What was a girl to do? The Americans were over here with money, and as I learned, treated them better than Aussie men did. They appreciated our courteous nature, such as holding the door. We hit it off, good for me. Susan told me of things to do during the day, and most evenings were ours.

I say most. On a particular Wednesday evening I went to a Sydney Club, The Motor Club. Sydney men are real drinkers, and many of the ladies also. The building was five stories high, restaurants and bars. The third floor was a Men's stag floor. Curious, I went in. It was loaded, perhaps 8PM. A long bar and tables. Waitresses carrying high, pitchers of beer. I pulled out some cash and worked my way to the bar. "Beer please, a tall one". Eyes turned toward me, taking measure. The fellow next to me asked if I was visiting, "Yes". "R&R?" He asked. He said he was an Australian Army Vet as his pitcher's arrived. He then asked, "What do you do". My response, "I'm a Spooky Gunship Pilot".

WHAT! And he lit up. "Come with me", and we walked over to a table where there were seven or eight other fellows. He announced that I was a Spooky Gunship Pilot, and the table erupted. "Make Room!" and a

112

chair was pulled up. They already had a couple of tables pulled together. They had been stationed near Saigon in an Australian contingent, and almost to a man told me that "Spooky had saved our ASSES many times". I never paid for another beer, as my glass was always filled.

Back in the day, I could drink beer. I must have there. But I think they served "3.2" beer, not much alcohol, because pitcher after pitcher were brought to the tables.

I guess I stayed a few hours, and finally said, "Time to Leave", and after hugs and slaps on the back, I was able to do so. They were the warmest men I have ever met, and a very pleasant Sydney memory.

The next day I took a bus out to "Bondi Beach", or something like that to take in the local scenery. The beach is a wide sandy beach, with modest waves. It was Fall down there so not many folks at the Beach.

I must make note of the women on the beach. Mostly one-piece suits, a few two piece, and no bikini's. Very conservative dress code. So, I got my day of sunshine, and back for an evening with Susan.

I felt the days slipping away and wanted to do it all. With Susan, I went by the old original prison, but gave up horseback riding. Susan must have had to work a couple of evenings, and on one of them I went to a dinner theater and was seated right up next to the stage. Being a "Cheeky" American, I interacted with some of the actors, and got some laughs. Fun all around.

LT COL GOOD SON

After a very pleasant R&R in Australia, I came back to find little changed. Major Ken Carpenter was not on the flight duty board.

I found my name associated with a new name as Aircraft Commander, Goodson, Lt Col. John Goodson. He was a new Squadron member. Col. Goodson was a career officer, Command Pilot, with over 20 year's service, and last duty was at the Pentagon. John and his wife resided in the Washington suburbs.

Col. Goodson was graying, about 5 feet eight, slender, and generally a warm personality. I didn't see him in the lounge area, he kept to himself. It was obvious he was an experienced, seasoned pilot and as I like to say, "Had good hands". Engine start, run-up, and takeoff went smoothly. We flew Saigon Caps as the Tet activity had quieted down. I only remember one significant action, and it was memorable.

We were flying CAP and we notified to support a Special Forces Long Range Patrol (LRP) Team. A LRRP Team was put into place as an observation team, combat capable, but not designed for attack. It typically consisted of a six or eight-man squad, all experienced, usually a Seal Team, Ranger or Green Berets.

Location coordinates were given, and it was in a usually hot area known as the "Angels Wing" The Angels Wing comes from map reading, where Cambodian Territory projects into Vietnam, with a "Nail head" shape. It was located on Hwy One, the Highway from the Cambodian Capital, Nom Penh, directly to Saigon.

Very significantly, it was the southern end of the Hoa Chi Min Trail. Cambodia, at the time was a "No-Go" area for US National political reasons, along with Laos. That restriction was lifted a few months later.

I had heard rumors of trucks lined up for a couple of miles, off-loading supplies there. Allied forces could not go after them because of our Rules of Engagement.

We made contact with the LRP Team, on our ARMY frequency FM radio. Communication was clear. They were on the move, pursued by the VC-NVA forces. They had been on recon observation.

Looking out at the darkness, I realized we were entering Cambodia. I half expected to see the dashed line on the ground indicating the border. The Navigator said nothing. I don't think we correlated the Vortac DME (Distance Measuring Equipment) to our position.

All of a sudden there was a furious outburst of tracer rounds accompanied by "Spooky, Get out! It's a trap!" "Go! Go!" from the FM radio. The LRP Team saw what was happening. The whole sky seemed to light up. I had already blackened the airplane, as was my standard practice, but perhaps there was a silhouette, in the night sky. All the fire was coming up in front of us, as Goodson entered a hard left bank. I could look out the left side windows, and see the firing positions. There were at least four of them, separated by about a thousand feet, a square.

"A Kill Box" entered my mind. Looking out my window to the front I could see the climbing rounds. They didn't wink out, but climbed to my estimate, to over 7,000 feet, twice our altitude. They were "ZPU", 14.7 millimeter, rounds. And between each tracer were at least five penetrating rounds. To this day, I believe each gun were at least dual barrels, perhaps quad. The cockpit was so brightly lit, I believe that one could have read a newspaper by the light.

In our turn, I said "Drop flare" and heard "Flare away". I began to count. "Ten, Nine, Eight …" to myself until I saw the flash of ignition. Again, I said "Drop flare" to have a second one dropped. I intended to take away their night vision.

Goodson saw them also, and as I looked left, and he was leaning over so far his head was below my shoulder. I made a now smart-ass comment "Where do you think you are going?" The plane had now reversed direction.

I called our situation a "Kill Box", and they were common along the Trail to the North, where they would shoot down Fast Movers Recon runs with their cross fire. Spooky's who were sent to the Trail during the early years (1966) and their crews just disappeared.

We were extremely lucky. The shooters were good, and I think the reason why the rounds were out in front of us was because we were slow. A faster airplane would have flown into the firing field. They could hear us, but really not see us. So, they just fired in the direction of our engines.

They had been trained to lead a plane, as they did, thus I saw real fireworks show.

If they had hit us, they would have brought us down. A ZPU round hit would have broken up our engines. If it hit the airplane, it would go through the bottom fuselage, through the floor and out the top. If a man was in the way, it would kill him.

Some might say, "Why didn't you shoot?" We would have been destroyed. We were no match. The 7.62 round is essentially anti-personnel, and our slant range, 3700 feet, would have used up its energy. If they were in range, Spooky would be in range.

Allow me to give examples. A 7.62 mm round is essentially the diameter of a pencil. A 50-caliber round is about the size of your index finger. A ZPU round is the size of your thumb. It would be no match.

I'd like to try to give you further information. Hold your right hand up in front of you with your thumb and fingers extended. Bring your left hand near with thumb folded and fingers extended. Hold them up in front of you. That is what the tracer pattern looked like. Now look up, and the ceiling represents the altitude of tracer wink out. Enough.

As we were exiting Cambodia, the Special Forces radio transmissions, was very apologetic. We reassured them we were ok. Shaken, but determined to help, we entered a pattern parallel to the border, out of range, and began dropping flares. The light helped the LRRP Team and they finally released us. The Army was going to cover them with night flares. We returned to Bien Hoa and never spoke of the experience.

I heard later that I was criticized for advocating withdrawal from the firing. My response "Were you there?" I never saw such ground fire ever again.

Col. Goodson and I flew three or four more CAP missions and I realized he was no longer on the board. I heard later he was transferred to Headquarters Nha Trang. He had come from the Pentagon, where I am sure he was an excellent Staff Officer, and yes, he could still pass a Flight Physical, but his night vision was gone. He had over twenty years of honorable duty, and probably more than one war. Those in charge were wise to allow him to finish his duty as a support officer, and return to the States at tour end, to years of retirement. I heard later of him through my parents and mutual mention of friends. Col. John, you had good hands.

LEFT-HANDED BRIDGE PLAYER

Major Frank L. Hines was a left-handed bridge player. He held his cards in his right hand and laid them down with his left. Many nights we played bridge to pass the time. He was good, and bid like me. He and I arrived in country about the same time.

It was about mid-way into my tour. I didn't know my brother's draft status, nor had I heard about my extension request. One of the benefits of a six-month extension is that you are given a free 30-day leave.

Sometimes things also just fall into one's lap. So it was that I got a second seven-day R&R. I thought about New Zealand, but only briefly. Sidney was too good for me. I wrote to Susan and told her I'd be returning. And so it was that I got to enjoy it all twice.

I was a floating Co-Pilot after my R&R and Goodson's departure. Frank Hines needed one, so he and I hooked up. Plus, he was now the Scheduling Officer, so we got to know our when's and where's, along with taking a Plane to Maintenance at Nha Trang on off days. We kept busy.

I have to relate another story. Saturday nights were always an active time. I used to say it was Vietnamese Payday every other Saturday, and the locals liked to shoot a couple of rockets into the Base after they had a few beers. Sort of Vietnamese Job Security. Intel had confirmed expected increased activity at the pre-flight briefing.

Four aircraft and crews were assigned each night. Spooky 71 took off at 6:30PM, with Spooky 72 on back up alert. Then Spooky 73 was to take off at 11:30PM, with Spooky 74 in reserve. This particular Saturday, we were scheduled on Spooky 73, the midnight assignment. So rather than inflight meals, a few of us decided to go to the new Mess Hall. It was a small group, which included a few men from Spooky 74, the late back up flight. We were relaxed and in a good mood.

The new mess hall replaced the old concrete building. It was quite spacious, with rows of tables, seating perhaps 12 people to a table. The single large room seated perhaps 300 people. The new building was all metal, with a high ceiling.

We entered the building after Pre-Flight, perhaps eight PM. We were the only ones there, and perhaps a little noisy. We went to the grill area and picked up our trays. There were two Airmen behind the grill.

A few at the front, myself included, said we wanted "Fried Eggs, three of them", and "We want fresh eggs". A Sargent approached and said "We are not doing that, you are having what we got", indicating this plastic pitcher that had an egg mix in it. To me they looked a little green. We said again, "We want fresh eggs, and break the shells". The bewildered Airmen just stood there. We were at an impasse.

"You Flyboy's come in here and think we are a catering kitchen" and "You'll take what we are serving". Someone leaned over and said "We are going to let the rockets in on you tonight". Hungry, with grumbling, we accepted the green poured egg mix on the grill. After served, we picked up the bacon, potatoes, toast, etc., and headed to a table. Actually, with a little hot sauce, the eggs were fine. But we were not satisfied.

We returned to Ops, and later made an on-time takeoff to our midnight posting Cap. About, 2AM we got an urgent radio message to return to Bien Hoa, rocket attack underway. We were there inside of twenty minutes from our Saigon Cap. The rocket launches were intermittent, and could be seen by the sparkle trail of the launch. We dropped a flare and received approval to fire into the expanded area of the launches off the end of the Runway.

The hot item for the VC were wrist watches and batteries. The rockets were fired remotely. The VC had lugged them all the way down from North Vietnam on the trail. An arduous task. But they did not have launching tubes. Instead, they would make wooden supports for the rockets, and hope for the best. Typically, they were the 107mm diameter rockets.

The hour hand on a watch was removed, and a small hole drilled in the plastic lens. This was hooked up to a battery, and when the minute hand touched the wire through the lens, the rocket ignited. The VC had gotten good at this method, and worked hard to get a battery and watch. None of the locals had a watch.

The VC had already departed our firing area. Our objective at shooting was to try to hit the tripod supporting the rocket and knocking it to the ground. Over the years, couple of crews had previously reported a little success, with a rocket motor igniting on the ground. But the attacks were light, perhaps twelve launches, and by the time we got there, they were all done.

The remainder of the night was quiet. We had expended our flares, and returned to land around five AM. A few of us were hungry by then and decided to get some breakfast. As we approached the serving line, we could see the Mess Sargent at a nearby table, holding his head. Looking up, he came over.

"Whatever you boys want; I never want to go through that again." Apparently, some of the rockets had landed nearby, and the noise inside the mess hall we heard was like a bass drum. That accompanied with a little shrapnel, had made an impression. The Airmen had a sly smile, reached under the grill area and pulled out cardboard trays with intact eggs. With the wave of the Sergeants hand, the Airmen started breaking them on the grill. We had fresh eggs.

The Sargent, who we figured was a new guy, then said "I have fresh bread coming out of the ovens, you want some?". Soon two cartons appeared with four or five loaves of bread, and blocks of butter. We split our bounty with the enlisted men to take back to quarters. A few of the officers were still up as we laid out the bread and found a serrated knife to cut the loaves, which was difficult to do because the bread was still fresh and warm. The butter had now softened, and was spread on the slices. They were delightful.

Every now and then we would have fresh bread courtesy of the Mess Hall to go along with our grilled steaks. Ah, combat life.

I think Major Hines liked me. A mutual respect, never complained. We had informational talk at our bridge table. The next subject was very enlightening. I never was a collector of "Hero" medals, but asked about them. His reply was "You have to write them up yourself". "What? You mean that nobody gets the nomination based on the mission?" Nope. Bien Hoa Flight did not have an Awards Officer. Now, if the Army sent in an accommodation report it may have been easier, as we often got "Day After" BDA (Bomb Damage Assessment), which were actually assigned body counts. I personally never liked them.

Career Officers need some medals to get promoted. I generally looked on them with jaundiced eye. It was almost impossible for a Co-Pilot to receive one as the honors would fall on the aircraft commander. With an AC's endorsement, I suppose one could get an award. Oh, there were Air Medals one could accumulate based on mission count. No writeups for the Nav's or Co-pilots.

The next subject was more upbeat. Hines said, almost as a side note that the Squadron had received an assessment for a pilot to go to Thailand on and extended TDY (Temporary Duty) assignment. Curious, I followed up with a "Tell me more". It would be to Udorn Air Force Base in Northern Thailand, and one would fly up into Laos ("Working on the Railroad"-Was the Slang) and support missions there. "Hmmm." Laos had not been opened up, but we had been supporting Laotians along the trail for years.

I did a little mental calculation. If I went TDY, I'd get my regular pay, combat pay, and the accompanying tax-free income, and adding in the TDY allotment, another $30 dollars a day. "I Asked how did one get the assignment?". The response, "Indicate you are interested". I was and said so.

About five days later, I received TDY orders for Udorn. I was now into my sixth month, April-May, with indefinite assignment. Was I being swept under the rug, I didn't know? I packed my gear, said a few goodbyes and off I went, somehow ending up in Udorn, where the life was entirely different, actually pleasant. No more rockets, mortars and weapons of war. I was assigned to live at a contracted city hotel, where my roommates at time to time were lizards near the night light. And the smells were entirely different, along with the street bustle. Taxi's were the way to get around, and dinners could be had at civilian restaurants.

I'll close this now. I had great adventures in Thailand and if this story's release is successful, I'll write up the next very interesting six months.

Oh, I caught up with Major Hines at our next assignment, and we had a nice couple of evenings together. He was assigned to B-52's. I did not see Major Carpenter for two years after the night of 25th of February 1969. He was on assignment at MacDill AFB, Florida. Several years later, I learned that Levitow had leukemia and died. I would have gone to see him in Connecticut. I have spoken with Sgt. Baer once, and he has a lot of resentment against the Air Force after his medical retirement. He felt abandoned by the military.

I have joined the Spooky Gunship Brotherhood organization and try to attend the annual reunions.

SPOOKY ADDENDUM

One particular day must have been in January. I was in the Ops trailer in the morning. Why? Who remembers? Anyway, there is this gnarly jet engine noise nearby, unlike any other. Quite loud. I opened the door and stepped out onto the stairs, and there in front of me, taxing by on what I considered just a road, was an all-black U-2 airplane, followed by a blue El Camino auto. Wow!

Our Ops area was near the east end of the runway. The U-2 would taxi by, make a left turn, and in a short time, be at the end of the runway. In less than a minute, the engine would roar, the airplane moved down the runway perhaps 800 feet, rotate, and raise the nose to a 30-degree climb angle, then to 45 degrees. The powerful engine drove it up until out of sight, inside the airbase boundary.

Meanwhile, the El Camino would run down the runway; someone would jump out and retrieve wing tip wheels, sort of like training wheels, that were designed to keep wings level through runway rotation. They were put in the open bay back, and the retriever got back in to drive off.

I did see, quite by chance, a recovery. The U-2 had centerline landing gear. By landing, the fuel had been depleted, so the plane sat higher. The blue El Camino appeared, with a couple of men in the back. They took the wheel to the wing tip and somehow loaded it. Then they went around to the other side and did the same. Sort of like a Nascar Pit Crew but with no jack. Once installed, the plane began to taxi, and the men got into the back of the car and followed the plane. All very efficiently done.

End.

SQUADRON MEMBERS—JUNE 30 1969 BIEN HOA, RVN

LTC Rowe, John J.

Maj Hines, Frank L.

Maj Bourgeois, Gerald F.

Maj Janssen, Larry D.

Maj Rentschler, James F.

Maj Fisher, James L.

Cpt Quill, Emmet C.

Cpt Archer, Robert P.

Cpt Gettis, Alanzo

Cpt Williams, Richard E.

Cpt Bessette, John F.

1Lt Polino, Gerald

1Lt Zinkievich, John M.

1Lt Peeples, David R.

1Lt Rose, Peter N.

1Lt Santelli, Stanley R.

1Lt. Slocum, Frank H.

1Lt. McClelland, Tom E.

1Lt. Harmon, Donald T.

1Lt. Bottema, Michael

1Lt. Moebes, William R.

1Lt. Cinquino, Mario A.

1Lt. McKee, Dean M.

2Lt. Westerfield, Melvin L.

2Lt. Olsen, Ronald B.

Msg Wecker, Harry H.

Msg Shropshire, William E.

Msg Cox David L.

Tsg Alley, Willie W.

Tsg Schilling, Robert C.

Tsg Hilton, Harold L.

Tsg Lester, joseph S.

Tsg Madole, Robert J.

Tsg Jedlica, Charles

Tsg Berryhill, Leo R.

Tsg Virden, Alfred E.

Ssg Fuzie, Edward

Ssg Williams, Tommy R.

Ssg Marley, Paul E.

Ssg Smith, Fred W.

Ssg Buckles Bobby E.

Ssg Mohgan, William A.

Ssg Levandowski, Edward F.

Ssg Goodwin, Terrance E,

Ssg Diaz, Vincent A.

Ssg Gilliam, Leroy

Sgt Smith, Paul D.

Sgt Keller, Jerry W

Sgt Saunders, Albert M

Sgt Beard, Richard P

Sgt Ramirez, Guillermo

Sgt Bailey, Warren H.

Sgt Horne, Dalton E.

Sgt Campbell, Herbert C

Sgt Foster, James R.

Sgt Weeden, George S.

Sgt Brooks, Ronald C.

A1C Blauvelt, James S.

A1C Trent, William E.

EPILOGUE

1) There was no burning flare. It would have destroyed the aircraft.

2) Major Ken Carpenter, Pilot, was rendered unconscious for two minutes by the concussion and flash. His first mission was as Aircraft Commander.

3) Had Lt. Frank Slocum, Co-Pilot, not taken control of the aircraft, it would have pitched up, rolled over, and impacted the ground in 20 to 25 seconds.

4) The loose flare may not have been attached to the cargo strap, nor had the safety been pulled.

5) A1C John Levitow first moved Sgt. Owen is away from the door. Had the flare timer been activated, the 15-foot parachute would have been ejected from the flared tube. This fact has never been reported.

6) It is most likely that A1C Levitow, struggling with the flare, simply threw it from the aircraft untethered.

7) Once leveled off, A1C Levitow reported "Smoking Flares" in the flare box.

He most likely suffered burns to his hands through his flight gloves as he lifted the smoldering flares from the box and pitched them out the door.

8) Sargent Baer suffered the gravest wounds to his right shoulder because he was closest to the exploding round and standing in the open fuselage.

9) The mortar round was most likely a South Vietnamese projectile that was fired before receiving a hold-fire notice, misunderstood, or disregarded.

10) All of the wounded received purple hearts. Baer received a medical discharge, Fuzie, Owen, and Levitow all returned to duty. No Award, Medal, or Commendation was issued to any other crew member.

Aircrew Members, Spooky 71

Major Kenneth L. Carpenter, Pilot

1st Lieutenant Frank H. Slocum, Jr., Co-Pilot

Major William P. Platt, Navigator

Staff Sargent Edward Fuzie, Flight Engineer

Sargent Thomas Baer, Gunner

Airman 1st Class Ellis C. Owen, Gunner

Airman 1st Class John L. Levitow, Loadmaster

Unknown Vietnamese Liaison

www.ingramcontent.com/pod-product-compliance
Lightning Source LLC
Chambersburg PA
CBHW060326050426
42449CB00011B/2676